UPSTAIRS
the PEASANTS
are
REVOLTING

ALSO BY DORCAS SMUCKER,

Ordinary Days: Family Life in a Farmhouse

UPSTAIRS
the PEASANTS
are
REVOLTING

More Family Life in a Farmhouse

Dorcas Smucker

Dorcas Smucker (signature)

Good Books

Intercourse, PA 17534
800/762-7171
www.GoodBooks.com

Acknowledgments

Special thanks to my family: Paul, Matt, Amy, Emily, Ben, Steven, and Jenny. You still love me even when I'm facing deadlines, you edit gently, and you seldom say, "Oh Mom, don't you dare put that in an article!"

Credits

All the essays in this book were published in *The Register-Guard*, Eugene, Oregon.

The scripture references on pages 44, 75, 90, and 104 are taken from the Holy Bible, New International Version® NIV®. Copyright © 1973, 1978, 1984 by the International Bible Society. Used by permission of Zondervan. All rights reserved.

The scripture reference on page 84 is taken from the Revised Standard Version of the Bible. Copyright © 1952 and copyright © 1946, by Division of Christian Education of the National Council of Churches of Christ in the United States of America. Used by permission. All rights reserved.

The scripture reference on page 154 is taken from the Holy Bible, King James Version.

The photo on page 168 is by Ellen Gerig. The photo on the back cover is by Amy Smucker.

Cover illustration and design copyright © 2007 by Wendell Minor.

Design by Cliff Snyder

Library of Congress Cataloging-in-Publication Data

Smucker, Dorcas.
    Upstairs the peasants are revolting : more family life in a farmhouse / Dorcas Smucker.
        p. cm.
    ISBN-13: 978-1-56148-600-7 (alk. paper)
    1. Country life--Oregon—Willamette River Valley—Anecdotes. 2. Farm life—Oregon—Willamette River Valley—Anecdotes. 3. Smucker, Dorcas—Family—Anecdotes. 4. Willamette River Valley (Or.)—Social life and customs—Anecdotes. 5. Willamette River Valley (Or.)—Biography—Anecdotes. 6. Mennonites—Oregon—Willamette River Valley—Biography—Anecdotes. 7. Spouses of clergy—Oregon—Willamette River Valley—Biography—Anecdotes. I. Title.
    F882.W6S56 2007
    979.5'3--dc22   2007026805

To my dad and mom,
Amos and Sara Yoder—

You taught me how to butcher chickens, save money,
disc a field, have fun, bake bread, keep learning,
talk "Dutch," write letters, can beans, tell stories,
feed lambs, fear God, and much more.
I love you both.

Table of Contents

HERITAGE AND HOPE

CHANGES AND A CHILD

Introduction

As an Amish child, I grew up as much on stories as on cornmeal mush and mashed potatoes. Shelling bushels of peas on the front porch, we listened to old family stories from Mom, scary stories from my brothers, memories, imitations, and quotes.

Today, as a somewhat more modern Mennonite minister's wife, I still, like my mother, feed my children mashed potatoes and stories. I repeat the ones I heard from Mom and turn our family escapades into tales to be repeated while washing dishes or snapping buckets of green beans on the front porch.

A story is much more than just a story, of course. It is entertainment, identity, interpretation, and lessons. This is who we are, this is why we do what we do, this is important, that is not, and don't ever whack your brother's finger with a hatchet like your dad did to Uncle Philip.

Writing essays about my life was a natural progression from storytelling. I write what I know: Oregon's Willamette Valley, growing grass-seed, our Mennonite church, my Amish past, our old farmhouse, my minister husband and six children. I have found what is true personally is also true universally. Even when the reader may be very different from me in location and lifestyle, we connect on the basics—friendship, family, laughter, grief, solving problems, faith in God.

The chapters in this book do not appear in chronological order and are meant to be read one at a time. I hope they remind you of stories in your own life, to be recalled and pondered and eventually retold.

Priorities and People

Barbells for my brain

My three-year-old daughter and I had a typical conversation the other morning. Jenny finished her breakfast and gave a satisfied belch. "Cereal makes me burp!" she announced, grinning. "And pop," she added.

"Pop?" I said.

"Pop makes me burp."

There was a short pause, then Jenny asked, "Does wine?"

"Wine?!"

"Does wine make me burp?"

"I...suppose it would."

"Every kind of wine?"

"Yes. Where did you hear about wine?"

"In my Bible storybook. There was a wedding party and there was wine."

Another pause, then another question.

"When I'm four years old am I gonna drink wine?"

"No."

"When I'm five can I?"

"Jenny," I said, "even Dad and I don't drink wine."

"Why not? Huh? Why don't you?"

"Because...um...you can get drunk if you drink wine."

"What's drunk?" she demanded.

I have been many things—dizzy, sick, pregnant, delirious— but never drunk.

"I think it's kind of like being dizzy," I finally said, feeling a bit dizzy with the pace of this conversation. To my relief, she dropped the subject, and I had a few minutes to recover before the next barrage of questions.

It was close to the same time that I started coming across suggestions for strengthening my mental abilities. "51 BRAINBOOSTING EXERCISES" an Internet link shouted at me. In *Reader's Digest*, I read, "Shake things up. When your brain is stimulated, new connections are thought to form between brain cells." It went on to encourage me to turn a book upside down and read it for three minutes, or to take a class, which would give me "more active brain cells."

The job of being a mom is sometimes perceived, among those who have never tried it, as a dull, unchallenging routine of washing dishes and wiping noses. But if being forced to think in new and different ways improves your brain, we moms may have the sharpest minds of anyone.

When adults ask me questions, their brains follow the same tracks as mine: "Are you busy on Friday?" "What news have you heard from your sister?"

Jenny, on the other hand, seldom thinks the way I do, and answering her questions is like driving a tractor across plowed furrows. She appears beside me when I'm typing an e-mail message and desperately whispers, "Mom! What's inside your lips?" When I'm studying a new lasagna recipe, she wants to know if the floors in heaven are brown. "How does rain make puddles?" she asks at the breakfast table—far too early, I think, for any conversation beyond "Pass the butter."

While three-year-olds ask the most questions, older children challenge my brain in different ways. Amy, who is 14, surveys the world around her and makes pithy observations that I would never have thought of. "This is the difference between Oregon and Minnesota," she told me, after a trip in December. "In Oregon, you say, 'My aunt has a broom.' And in Minnesota you say, 'My aahhnt has a brum.'" I couldn't have put it better myself.

Twelve-year-old Emily is an expert at what I call CBS (Clear Blue Sky) questions that force me to ask a dozen questions in return to figure out what she's talking about. "How old was that Amish lady?" for example. Or, "What was that guy's name?"

"Take a class," *Reader's Digest* instructed me. If learning new facts gives me more active brain cells, my two boys must keep my neurons snapping like a bag of Orville Redenbacher's in the microwave.

Both Matt and Ben have had a series of obsessions, where they were stuck on one subject for a year or more and that consumed all their thoughts and conversations. And they could never seem to process what they learned unless they ran every detail by me first.

Matt began with animals, and I'll never forget the morning he wandered sleepily into the kitchen and greeted me with, "Do you know what has the largest eyes of any land mammal? The horse!" Thanks to Matt, I learned about the relative size and habitat of the anaconda vs. the boa constrictor, the feeding habits of the Madagascar hissing cockroach, and the gestation period of the African elephant.

A few years ago Matt left animals behind and became fascinated with astronomy. He taught me that if I visited the planet Saturn, not only would I be unable to move around because I'd weigh so much, but I'd sink down into it because Saturn is actually a ball of compressed gas.

When NASA sent a small probe to an asteroid some time ago, I suggested to Matt that instead of trying to be the first man on Mars, he should be the first one on an asteroid. Somehow it seemed safer. "That wouldn't work, Mom," he said. "An asteroid is so small that I'd obtain escape velocity just by jumping." What a thought.

Ben has passed through the geography phase, when he read atlases by the hour and kept me informed on how much the population of Calcutta had increased in the past 10 years. Now, at nine, he is into sports. Just in the last few days I've learned that Shaq was six-feet-six when he was 13 years old, that Magic Johnson made $500 million in his career, and that "Arizona State University and the United States have one thing totally opposite—one is ASU and the other is USA!"

I wonder what I'll do to keep my mind sharp when they all grow up and leave home. Maybe then I'll have to read a book upside down through my bifocals or go back to school.

Or maybe, if I'm really fortunate, I'll have a few three-year-old grandchildren.

For better, for worse

I don't know if it was the laughter or the vomiting that made that night unforgettable, but I look back on it as one of the finest moments of our marriage.

We had been married for three-and-a-half years, and I was pregnant with our second child. A vicious stomach flu was going around, and Paul had spent the day curled up in bed, his face a delicate shade of green. I don't know if I had the flu or not, because, being pregnant, I was throwing up a dozen times a day, every day.

That evening, we tucked Matthew, who was almost two, into his crib, and then we went to bed. About 1 a.m., I heard Matthew retching in the next room. I rushed over to help him, but one whiff sent me flying for the bathroom, where I threw up into the toilet.

So Paul dragged himself out of bed and soon Matthew lay whimpering on our bed, Paul stood at the sink miserably rinsing sheets, and I continued to lean over the toilet, gagging.

When everything was cleaned up, we went back to bed, with Matthew in bed between us. Half an hour later, the whole depressing scene was repeated.

Soon, Matthew once again lay whimpering on our bed, Paul rinsed out more sheets, and I continued to heave into the toilet. We were almost ready to go back to bed when suddenly the whole pathetic situation struck us funny.

We stood in our cold bathroom, pale and thin and sick, holding onto each other for support, laughing and laughing.

I am remembering this sort of thing these days for two reasons. First of all, our anniversary on August 10 always makes me nostalgic, and, secondly, Paul and I were asked to give premarital counseling to Konrad and Shannon, a newly engaged young couple we know.

We consented, of course, but wondered how to distill the hard-won experience of 19 years into a capsule of wisdom to give them at this crucial time in their lives, how to prepare them for the inevitable tough times ahead.

With marriages dissolving all around like sugar cubes in hot coffee, launching a young man and woman into matrimony is a serious undertaking. We soon realized that there was no way we could tell them everything we've learned. We could, however, draw a few basic lessons from our own experiences to give them a solid foundation.

We also evaluated, as best we could, their readiness for marriage and were happy to find that they were better prepared than we had been. Most of all, we wanted them to know what love really is, that marriage is bigger than the two people involved, and that a firm commitment can keep them together even in the hard times.

Love has many definitions but too often, we feel, it is portrayed as nothing but a capricious emotion. I went to college with a young woman whose husband was in the military. After he came back from a tour of duty overseas, she said, "I was afraid that when John came home I wouldn't love him anymore."

"You mean, don't you, that you were afraid he wouldn't love you anymore?" I asked.

"No," she said. "I was afraid I wouldn't love him anymore."

Seriously considering marriage at that time, I was horrified at the thought of having no control over whether or not I loved my husband. Thankfully, I learned that love is primarily a decision and a commitment. No matter how we feel, we can choose to love—to honor, to value highly, to be there, to sacrifice for and listen to.

And paradoxically, in this mundane soil of duty and forgiveness and unselfishness, feelings of love and romance are safe to sprout and grow.

As we talked with Konrad and Shannon, out by our picnic table, it was obvious that they were in love. (Konrad, I'm told, is especially obsessed, and has been known to pull Shannon's photo out of his pocket and show it to perfect strangers.) We asked them, "Which of you tends to be more emotional?" and they looked at each other, exploring the universe in each other's eyes for a long minute before they answered.

But it was also obvious that their love is built on more than their feelings. They were friends first, and Konrad was pretty sure that Shannon was who he wanted to marry. Yet, before he ever asked her out, he did some clearheaded and unromantic research, much like a prospective employer checking out references. He talked to Shannon's parents, her pastor, her friends, even her old high-school principal. After they began dating, he encouraged her to do the same with people who knew him well.

"I like it," Shannon said. "The more people I talk to, the safer I feel. It's like we have all these people behind us, supporting us."

This sense of belonging to a community was important to us as well. I have often felt reassured knowing that our family and friends are rooting for us, a safety net to catch us. At the same time, I know that the success or failure of our marriage will ultimately affect everyone around us.

We also were impressed with Konrad and Shannon's ability to communicate. It amazes me at times that Paul and I are still happily together, considering how much we had to learn when we got married. Our communication skills were poor, and in many areas we had little in common.

But what gave us a framework to work things out was a rock-solid commitment to this marriage. Not only was our marriage part of a bigger community, it also was a separate entity, somehow larger than the two of us put together. We learned that it was worth sacrificing our own wishes for the good of the marriage.

We also took seriously the biblical concept that God intended marriage to be for life, and even if the other partner bailed out, we would be stuck with our vows until death, which made a powerful incentive to work things out. Since marriage was God's idea, we knew he wanted it to work even more than we did, which was wonderfully reassuring when we seemed unable to find solutions on our own.

Nineteen years later, I consider my husband to be one of the best gifts I have ever received, and our marriage an environment where I can be myself and grow as a person like nowhere else.

Our feelings for each other change from day to day. Sometimes we love each other with a warm friendship, sometimes we're sky-high "in love," and sometimes we really don't like each other very much at all. But our emotions do not change the basic commitment to our marriage.

This is what I want for Konrad and Shannon—a loving and joyful marriage that brings out the best in both of them. And, since difficult times are inevitable, I also want to see them determined to face those times together. As bizarre as it is, I wish for them the kind of experience we had that dreadful night in 1988.

Falling in love is nice, and staying there is better. But to have someone committed to being there and laughing with you when life hits bottom—it doesn't get much sweeter than this.

For today, all is forgotten

oeing in the garden one afternoon last week, I found a nice-sized green apple lying in a corn row. Hmmmm, how odd, the orchard is a long way from the garden. I had inventoried my apple supply just the day before and realized what a meager crop was out there. We would be doing well to get a dozen quarts of applesauce, and we needed four times that much. So why was one of my precious apples lying in the garden?

I began investigating, and soon the reluctant truth came out. That morning, Ben and Steven, our two middle-sized boys, had finished weeding the hedge. Ben loves to play softball, so he suggested they have some batting practice. Furthermore, he got the bright idea to pick apples and see if they could hit them across the fence into the clover field.

"How many did you pick?" I gasped.

Oh dozens, maybe?

We will draw the curtain of charity over the rest of the scene, as Mark Twain once said, except to say that the boys' punishment was greatly reduced by a strategical error on my part. I called my husband Paul for support and sympathy, and he started laughing. "I understand them so well," he said, "because when I was a kid, I would spend hours hitting a rock over the clothesline with a broomstick."

The prosecution thought this was irrelevant, but the judge overruled, and the boys received a reduced sentence of digging an extra half-hour beside the carport where we're putting gravel in, plus a warning that they will pay for an equivalent amount of apples if I have to buy any to make applesauce.

I should be used to this sort of thing, as Ben is at the age when a boy seems to be all noise and awkward angles and disaster. He rattles the kitchen lights below him when he jumps out of bed or shoots baskets in his room, he drapes over chairs like a discarded bathrobe, and he seems to have forgotten how to actually sit upright. "But that's the whole point," he sighs when I tell him to stop doing things that make his sister scream.

But today, all my frustrations with him are forgiven and almost forgotten. Today, I am oozing with hugs and nostalgic affection. Today is Ben's birthday, and he's 12 years old.

I feel this same surprise with every child's birthday: How on earth can he be this old already, and where has the time gone? How did Ben change so quickly from a cuddly little guy with a phenomenal head of dark hair into this young man with his first pimple who in just the last few months has come up to my chin, my nose, and now my eyes?

On each birthday, I reminisce about the labor and delivery. "You sure took your sweet time about coming!" I tell Ben. "Your dad and I walked the halls of that little hospital for hours. I wore this pink and purple bathrobe that I made myself and it was so pretty."

"Interesting," Ben says, his catch-all word for "I am trying to be polite here but this really does not interest me in the least."

From there, I recount everything Ben has survived to reach this age. I recall the time he was the last child I pulled out of a van that had caught fire, the time he dumped camphorated oil on his head and into his mouth and had to have his stomach pumped, and the time he and his sister wandered off down the creek and got lost.

He has a 12-year collection of scars. One can still see where he fell down the steps and put his tooth through his lip, and a vivid white scar on his head shows us where his sister lost her temper and hit him with a bag of wood scraps and nails.

But somehow, by God's grace, he's made it to 12 years old.

Actually, as Ben pointed out to us last evening, standing by the piano and lecturing in his yellow-and-red pajamas, he was going to be 12 years old at 10:12 p.m. the night before we celebrated his birthday, since he was born at 12:12 a.m. in Ontario, Canada, which is two hours ahead of Oregon.

"Yes, Ben," we said. "You're absolutely right." Ben is the most technical and mathematical of a long line of technical Smuckers, and we have learned not to argue details with him.

In my estimation, Ben has been a math phenomenon ever since he came to me at age seven and said he had multiplied 128 times 128 in his head and it was 16,384. I grabbed a calculator and checked. He was right. Having such genius in the house scared me for about two days. Then when I saw he was still whining about green beans for supper and absentmindedly putting the paper towels in the refrigerator, I knew he was still the kid we knew and loved.

Ben's statistics keep us all informed and entertained. "There's this baseball player that has a 10-year, $252 million contract. That's $25.2 million a year! At one point, it was more than the salary of the entire Tampa Bay Devil Rays team put together!"

"I bet if you had a list of the world's 25 tallest mountains, most of them would be in Asia because, like, there's the

Himalayas and then in Kazakhstan there's some that are over 24,000 feet."

Dealing with a telemarketer, he spouts, "Sorry, we do not have a TV and I realize there's only two percent of American households that don't have a TV, so bye!"

We never know what Ben will do or say next, whether he will make us laugh or learn or tear out our hair. But as his mom, I do know he has a few special statistics of his own—he is my second boy, my fourth child, the one who looks the most like me and acts the most like his dad, yet there's no one else quite like him.

Tomorrow, I may tune Ben out when he quotes basketball numbers, grieve a bit for those apples, or yell upstairs in annoyance when the kitchen lights jangle like Salvation Army bells at Christmas time.

But not today. Today is Ben's birthday, and I have a long-range perspective: It's been a good 12 years.

Fresh perspectives

There were seven of us in the boat, pulling in crab rings—Paul, me, and five boys from 10 to 12 years old. We motored under the bridge at Waldport, its enormous concrete mass arching over us and tapering away to the south like the tail of a gigantic lizard. Cormorants and seagulls rested on a crossbar, staring at us, annoyed, as though we had interrupted a family reunion.

"Wow," the boys said. "It's way different down here than seeing it from on top."

Like looking up at a bridge from down below, Bible Memory Camp let us see life from a different angle and thoroughly enjoy ourselves at the same time.

It all began many years ago when my husband Paul memorized Bible verses so he could go to White Branch Camp in the Cascades. Years later, he found himself pastoring with a fellow camper, Arlen Krabill, and they decided to give the children in their church the same opportunity they had had.

So every year, they specify 50 Bible verses, and any child between the ages of nine and 14 who memorizes them all gets to go to camp for three days. It isn't a specific church camp like the old days, but in tents at Clear Lake, in a house at the coast, or horseback riding in the Cascades.

This year, 15 of us went to a house in Waldport—Arlen and his wife Sharon, Paul and me, a teenaged counselor, and 10 campers. The house had only one bathroom, which, since this age does minimal grooming, was not a huge hardship.

The kids, I'm sure, saw an entirely new side of their pastors, who are usually dark-suited and behind the pulpit. One day, Arlen wore a T-shirt festooned with promises written in childish handwriting. "I promise not to sleep in church, especially during the sermon ... I promise not to sing off key and always arrive on time ... I never chew gum in church or sneak out early. Because I am the minister."

"My son gave it to me," he explained.

Sharon, normally a model of dignity, hiked up her skirts and raced one of the boys down the beach. (He won, barely.) Paul told stories around the campfire of his own camp days, how his dad was a counselor (Grandpa Smucker?), and some of the older boys picked him up and tossed him into the swimming pool (No! Grandpa?) and he calmly swam to the other side. (Grandpa can swim?)

Mostly, we just had fun. This age group, post potty-training and pre-acne, throws itself into every activity with the wild enthusiasm of running into the ocean and leaping the waves.

As a mom, it was good to see how perfectly normal my two middle children are with their love of heated debate and their crazy sense of humor.

The campers argued endlessly for the sheer joy of arguing. Is it smart or dumb to stay up all night at a sleepover? "It's dumb!" Emily said. "You're grouchy the next day."

"You're not grouchy if you sleep all the next day," Preston insisted.

"You get to see the sun rise! And you get to see Mars!" Ben added.

The girls went through all the chants they know, slapping each other's hands in perfect rhythm. "I don't WANna go to MEXico no more, more, more."

"That's dumb," Justin said.

"It takes coordination!" Amy snapped back.

"Guys are more coordinated than girls!"

"Then let's see you do that!"

"If girls are so coordinated, how come they can't dribble a basketball as well as guys?"

I saw my son's sense of humor multiplied by five. Dan set his breakfast plate on the picnic table one morning and went back for orange juice. Justin filched Dan's muffin and hid it in his lap. Dan returned, looked at his plate, and said, "Hey, I thought I had a muffin!" He shrugged his shoulders and went back for another one.

Giggling hysterically, the other guys replaced his muffin. Dan came back and they all howled with laughter. Dan just sighed.

They also thought the Billy Bass fake fish on the wall was hilarious. He could swivel out from the wall and croak "Take Me to the River" half a dozen times a day, and still someone would want to sneak over and push that little button to make him sing still more.

Nine of the kids came from solid, well-fed, two-parent homes. The tenth was Sergey, the wild card in the deck and the puppy in the henhouse. A tough, wiry little 12-year-old from Moscow, he spent the summer with another camper's family and memorized his verses in Russian.

Sergey's vague history included abandonment, hunger, and fighting for survival. As frenzied and pesky as a fly in a tent, he was nevertheless a lovable child.

The boys "crabbed" from the dock one day while the girls took their turn out in the boat. Paul helped Sergey tie his rope to the dock and toss out the crab ring. "Wait at least five minutes before you haul it in," he said.

"Five minutes? How much is five minutes?" Sergey asked. Obviously, almost forever. He paced up and down the dock, grabbing my wrist every 15 seconds to check the time. "Is it five minutes? Huh? Is it? Yeah, it is, see? It's at the one!"

"No, it isn't," I said. "It's still on the 12."

"But there's a one there! See?"

"That one is part of the 12!"

He dropped my wrist in agonies of impatience.

"What's 'one' in Russian?" I asked, desperate to distract him.

"*Ah-deen.*"

"Two?"

"*Dvah.*"

He counted, I repeated. "*Dree, tishtee,*" and on through the complicated consonants to 10. Then he grabbed my wrist again. "Is it five minutes? Yeah, it's five minutes!"

For the children, everything was an adventure: the edge-of-their-seats memory-verse contest (won by the girls), the sand sculpture contest (won by Emily and Kayla's train coming out of a tunnel), and the late-night charades ("Jack and the Beanstalk," featuring Destinie as Jack).

No one complained about kitchen cleanup, even when Katie, the quietest girl, and Sergey, the noisiest boy, had to wash dishes together.

After camp, Sharon went home, fell asleep at 8 p.m., and slept all night. Paul turned the grass-seed cleaners back on at the warehouse. I filled a box with pillows and socks left behind in our van. Sergey flew back to Moscow.

"Thank you for investing your valuable time in the campers," Katie's mom wrote in a thank-you note. "I know there are many other things you could have been doing."

Perhaps, but I can't think of anything better I could possibly have done with those three days.

Simply complicated

Sometimes living simply gets very complicated.

The first batch of corn this summer wasn't large, less than a hundred ears. But it was terribly wormy and processing it seemed to take all day.

The children did the husking on the front porch, just outside the kitchen. Every few minutes I heard a shriek as an ear of corn went flying back into the basket and my teenage girls sat rigidly with huge round horrified eyes, their hands splayed stiffly in the air as though they were geckos climbing a wall.

"Oooooh, now that one wins the prize!" they exclaimed, their voices shaking. Then they would draft 11-year-old Ben to drop the offending brown caterpillar down the gaps in the porch floor.

I helped with the husking for a while, gingerly pulling back the silk to check for the brown granules that indicate worms, then quickly whacking off the end of the ear with a sharp knife. When I was too slow, I shuddered just like my daughters as one of the biggest larva specimens I had ever seen humped its way out of the ear.

After the husking came more endless jobs—blanching the corn, batch by batch; cooling it in buckets filled from the garden hose; and then cutting the corn off the cobs.

When the last bag of corn was finally in the freezer, I scrubbed the kitchen, chiseling dried bits of corn from the floor and counters. We counted the day's total; from all that work and anguish, we reaped a measly 11 quarts of corn, only a small fraction of what we need for the winter.

I wondered, Was it worth it?

This is the sort of dilemma I face daily, trying to balance my limited resources of time, energy, and money to serve God, help others, live simply, and provide the best sort of life for my family. Most of us long for simplicity, for a less hectic life with more time, peace, and fulfilment. Often, people see the Amish as living this sort of ideal life.

"I've always thought I would like to be Amish," a man in the blueberry patch told me wistfully this summer. "So far, my wife hasn't been willing, but I would be happy to get rid of our modern things and join the Amish."

These people also see me, with my Amish roots, as uniquely qualified to prioritize my life and center on what's really important. While those roots taught me practical skills and the value of family and community, I find myself somewhere between my Amish past and the modern world.

Many of my mother's choices were defined by her church community and by poverty. Living in a different era, I have to define my own priorities and weigh hundreds of options my mother never had.

I believe in sacrificing lesser things to gain greater, in putting people before things, in family and community over self, in God's kingdom over all. I believe in homegrown over store-bought, in natural over artificial, in homemade over manufactured.

Even with these well-defined priorities, I constantly face tough choices.

Is it okay to buy a fast-food meal if it means more time with a friend? If having a garden means I don't have time to teach vacation Bible school, which do I choose? Is making my own food always better than buying it? Am I insisting on doing things the slow and old-fashioned way long after it becomes pointless? Can I use Bug-B-Gon to keep those disgusting worms off the corn?

And what about those green beans last week? Only about a third of my green bean seeds sprouted this year. The plants produced lavishly, but I ended up with only 10 quarts of beans, about a fourth of what I wanted. I couldn't bear to feed my family tasteless supermarket canned beans all winter, so I found a produce stand that sells fresh beans and ordered 30 pounds. For an extra 25 cents a pound, they told me, they could cut and wash them for me.

"Sure," I said impulsively, thinking of efficiency and time saved, and took home three large plastic bags of stiff, moist, green bean pieces. When I hauled them into the kitchen and set them on the counter, five-year-old Jenny burst into tears. "But I like to snap beans, Mom. Didn't you get any that I can snap for you?"

I tried to comfort her, explaining that I had so much to do, my sister was coming to visit in two days, I really needed to can the applesauce as well, and this was a nice way for me to save some time. But my explanation fell flat. How could saving time possibly matter to a five-year-old when she loves to snap beans?

My state of mind did not improve when I was imprisoned in the kitchen for several hours while I monitored two pressure canners full of beans, terrified that either my absentmindedness or my temperamental stove would blow up the house.

By the time I pulled the last jars from the canners, I still didn't know exactly what I should have done. If my garden beans didn't do well, should I do what my mother would have done and serve extra cabbage salad all winter instead of beans? Did it make sense to buy and can beans that someone else grew, or was that as pointless as making a pie with a purchased pie crust and instant pudding?

Should I buy fresh beans at Safeway every now and then all winter? Or would beans in tin cans ultimately be the best use of my time and money?

I sensed, however, that if I were going to buy beans, it would have been better to buy them whole instead of cut, that the experience of having the family snap them together would have been more important than the time I saved.

Like everyone else, I wish for a defined and tranquil life, but it doesn't look like I'll ever get it. Come to think of it, in many ways my mother's life wasn't so ideal, either. She worried constantly about our finances, and when the pigs got into the garden, Mom was as stressed and frantic as any suburban mother running late in slow traffic. But today she knows that, for the most part, she chose the things that mattered over the things that didn't.

Meanwhile, I still aim for simplicity and face daily dilemmas in how to achieve it, but I allow myself to make mistakes on the way.

Doing the corn, I've decided, was a good idea even though we got only 11 quarts. Years from now, the girls will shudder and laugh together, remembering a goal accomplished, those dreadful worms, and a heroic little brother gently dropping them down the gaps in the porch floor.

Finding common ground

My daughter Emily carefully set the bottle of ink on the table in our room at Motel 6. Next, she opened a narrow box and removed an elegant writing instrument, too classy to be called a mere pen—a spiraling length of heavy green glass that narrowed to a clear, grooved tip. Slowly, she dipped it into the ink and began to write on a yellow legal pad.

Sprawled on the bed, I watched her briefly and then returned to reading my book.

Some time later, Emily pressed her new blotter on the words, then slowly folded the paper, walked toward me, and bowed. "A letteh for yew, Madahm," she announced, in a contrived accent.

I opened it and read.

Once upon a time, there was a girl named Emily. Emily had a big family. Sometimes Emily felt that her parents didn't love her. One day Emily came out of school and a robber grabbed her. She kicked and screamed. The kidnapper was her mom! Emily's mom dragged Emily clear across the country. And I don't know what happened next, cause I'm Emily and I am still being held hostage!

Emily Smucker

P.S. I don't feel unloved anymore.

The "letter" was quintessential Emily, an imaginative mix of fantasy and reality, of elegant handwriting and splotches of ink, of clarity and confusion.

We have a custom in our family of taking each child away by themselves—I take them when they're 12, Paul when they're 13. But I had never taken Emily on what the children call a Twelve Trip, since she had serious health issues when she was 12, and at 13 we were preoccupied with going to Africa for the winter.

When she reached 14, the time was right. What should I do with her? A few years earlier, I took her older sister Amy to Portland on the train and went shopping. Emily doesn't like it when I compare her to her calm and responsible sister, and yet she constantly compares my treatment of the two of them and resents it if I don't treat them equally.

I would take Emily shopping as well, I decided, at Woodburn's outlet mall and in the historic town of Silverton. I did the train thing with Amy, so I would do something different with Emily. Something dramatic for the drama queen. I would kidnap her.

Paul made motel reservations and agreed to take care of things at home. I made arrangements with Emily's teacher.

I wore sunglasses and a long trench coat with upturned collar when I arrived at school on a Friday afternoon to whisk her away. I didn't play the part nearly as well as Emily would have. In fact, I looked like a 40-something mom making a fool out of herself. Emily would have snapped into the role perfectly, skulking along with sinister mystery in every step.

She is a born actress—always playing a part—who can whirl a piece of fabric around her shoulders and suddenly become Queen of the Smuckers, tall and haughty. "Bow before me," she commands, so regal that we feel a strange compulsion to do just that. The next day, she impulsively turns a piece of masking tape into a moustache and suddenly she is a science teacher, pompously lecturing in the middle of an otherwise normal afternoon.

Who is Emily, really? I often wonder. What is merely a role she plays and what is reality? Is she a cute little girl or an elegant young woman? Is she simply playing at being a "typical" teenager, moods shifting with the winds, angry and unreasonable one day and thoughtful and understanding the next? Is she actually the wise and witty young woman who has a special sensitivity for older people and small children?

For some time now, our relationship has been the same sort of mixture as the letter she wrote—impulsive affection and arguments, miscommunication, and moments when our eyes meet with an electric current and we instantly understand each other.

The purpose of our trip was not only to affirm and honor Emily, but to get to know her better. We have been through times when our communication looked like a geometry diagram of two separate lines in two different planes, neither parallel nor intersecting, with no shared points.

But slowly, we are finding things we have in common. I am a bookworm; she was the child who struggled to read. And then one day she discovered the delicious thrill of words, reading Robin Hood and quoting aloud, "'Hark! Yonder cometh a gaily feathered bird,' quoth Jolly Robin." She looked at me and grinned, and I grinned back, both of us getting the same buzz from the old-fashioned words.

We both love classic elegance, and fell in love with the glass pens at our first stop that Friday, an antique shop. She couldn't believe I would buy one for her, as much as they cost. "This is your day," I said, deliberately setting aside my tightwad tendencies.

"The owners told me that if someone is deserving, I can add a blotter besides," the clerk told us. Emily chose a blotter with pictures of antique ink bottles and Italian text.

Shopping at Gap was rapture for Emily and torture for me, digging through a wasteland of flimsy scraps of fabric that in my opinion hardly qualified as clothes. But I kept my opinions to myself and amazingly, we found an outfit that fit my strict parameters, and I bought Emily a shirt, skirt, and shoes.

We spent the night in Salem, and on Saturday we wandered around Silverton, admiring the murals and historic brick buildings. We walked around one block twice before we found the tea shop we were looking for, entered it, and found ourselves in the most charming atmosphere we could have imagined. The waitresses wore little black hats and long, full skirts, and the tea was served in miniature pots bundled in quilted cozies. The desserts were pure elegance, lemon tart for Emily and a Belgian chocolate torte for me, complete with a fresh nasturtium on the plate.

One thing we completely understand about each other is our sheer joy in places like this. We savored the flavors and atmosphere for an hour, and then it was time to go home.

"Do you really feel like we don't love you?" I asked, her "letter" gnawing at my mind.

Emily laughed and hugged me. "No, I was just being silly. I know you love me."

She was soon asleep, a tall and lovely young woman curled up on the seat like a small child—no roles, no pretense, just Emily, herself. I drove home in the pouring rain, thinking of how much I love her and how blessed I am to be her mom.

The indispensable mom

*E*rma Bombeck once wrote that if she had her life to live over again, she would go to bed with a cup of tea when she was sick instead of acting like the world would go into a holding pattern if she wasn't there to direct it.

Normally I agree with Erma, but at the time, as I clipped and filed the quote, I wasn't sure. Did we moms choose to make ourselves irreplaceable, or was it part of the job description? Could my family's world keep turning if I stayed in bed the next time I was sick?

I had a chance to test Erma's philosophy. One Friday evening, I first sensed that all was not well when a dull ache crawled up my arms and my head slowly grew five pounds heavier. I went to bed and shivered for half an hour before falling asleep.

Just after midnight, the soft swish of flannel pajamas woke me. Beside the bed stood 11-year-old Ben. "Mom, I threw up."

He was calm and clean. Wonderful, I thought. He's 11. He knows how to run for the bathroom, no big deal.

"Oooooh, that's too bad," I murmured, half asleep. "Why don't you take a bucket, just in case, and go back to bed?"

"I threw up all over my blankets."

I shook Paul. "Ben threw up."

He slept on, his good ear conveniently down in the pillow and his deaf ear up. Only Gabriel's trumpet could wake him before Ben's bed would be soaked to the mattress.

Erma meant well, I'm sure, but her husband must have been a light sleeper.

We plodded upstairs, and I gingerly pulled the blankets off the loft bed six inches above my head. Walking across Interstate 5 in the dark would feel less risky than this.

Ben was surprisingly eager to help. "I can stuff the blankets in the hamper, Mom," he offered. Holding my breath as I gathered the corners of the blankets to contain the mess, I didn't answer. He tried again. "Shall I put them in the hamper for you?"

So this is the legacy I have left my children—the idea that everything you put in a laundry hamper, even something as unspeakable as those blankets, is magically restored to its clean and rightful glory by some good fairy.

"No, no," I sighed, "just get a clean blanket and go back to bed. With a bucket."

On Saturday, I had a long list of chores to accomplish. I wasn't sick, really, and surely after I had another cup of tea, it wouldn't be such hard work to open my eyes, and walking across the kitchen wouldn't feel like wading in peanut butter.

By noon, I was leaning against the sink, exhausted and chilled. Fourteen-year-old Emily looked at me and commanded, "Mom, just go to bed!"

Was Erma speaking through my daughter? "All right," I said. "I give up." I stretched out on the recliner with a wool blanket around me while Emily, bless her, mopped the kitchen.

My temperature slowly percolated upward, my breathing grew more painful, and I started to fall asleep, an invisible signal for everyone to crowd into the living room to ask me questions.

The three youngest were hungry. Paul was taking a load of donations to St. Vincent de Paul for me. Amy and Emily were going to shop for groceries.

"Mom! What's for lunch?"

"Where's your wallet?"

"Okay, so what besides the old dryer did you want me to take?"

"I'm hungry."

"How much money do we need?"

"Is the brown stove ready to load up?"

"Okay, so to get to WinCo, you go down 99 and then where? Beltline or something?"

"What's for lunch?"

"Have you seen my new jacket?"

"Were there some Goodwill bags or something you wanted me to take, too?"

"Shall I make macaroni and cheese?"

"If I don't get the new dryer hooked up until Monday, are you going to have enough clean school uniforms?"

At last they left me alone and I curled up miserably under the blanket.

My fever was inching higher, I was sure of it. The pain in my chest was getting worse, and if all went well, a full-blown case of pneumonia would send me to the hospital where I could sleep all I wanted and no one would bother me except doting nurses in quiet shoes coming to take my temperature and bring tea.

The phone rang. Amy answered and hollered to me, "Dad's wondering if the Goodwill bags can go to St. Vincent de Paul."

You've got to be kidding me, I thought. "That was the idea," I croaked. Amy repeated it into the phone, and hung up. "Guys!" she muttered.

These people, I decided, would not survive without me.

Sunday morning I stayed home from church, too sick to go away but not too sick to make lunch for my beloved family who always comes home famished after church. Alternately working and resting for 10 minutes, I made my usual chicken and rice hot dish and a salad. I sensed guiltily that this was the sort of heroic-mom stuff Erma regretted at the end of her life.

My heroics did not extend to dishes, so Paul and the children washed them while I stayed in bed. Feeling worse instead of better, I gratefully sank my head in the pillow, closed my eyes, and fell asleep. Once again, this signaled my younger children to swing open the bedroom door, one after another, like cuckoos popping out of a clock.

"Can I have a piece of bubble gum?"

"Me, too?"

"What shall I do? There's no more bubble gum in the jar."

"Mom! Steven took a piece of candy without asking. I saw him hide the wrapper."

"Can I go outside?"

That did it. Since when, I asked them, does anyone in this house have to ask if they can go outside on a Sunday afternoon? And why weren't they pestering their dad with all these questions instead of me?

Dad, it turned out, was taking a nap on the couch. They didn't want to bother him.

I sent them outside and burrowed under the blankets. My lungs hurt, my head hurt, and I could no longer remember why I had ever gotten married, let alone had six children. Don't they put pneumonia patients under a tent in the hospital? How lovely to be all alone under a dreamy white tent with no sound but the burble of Vicks-y steam rising from a vaporizer.

On Sunday evening, someone found a box of ice cream sandwiches left to melt on a kitchen chair. Emily couldn't remember if she had a clean uniform for the next day, and Jenny's nails, I discovered, were awfully long because no one had thought of trimming them.

"Paul," I said, "I have failed as a mom."

"You have?"

"I have made myself indispensable. A good mom works herself out of a job, but you guys can't function without me."

Paul looked at me like my fever was higher than he had realized. "You're supposed to be indispensable."

"I am?"

"We need you. If we didn't need you around, what would be the point of being a mom?"

"I don't know," I said.

Nevertheless, when Ben threw up again a few nights later, I elbowed Paul until he woke up. "Your turn," I smiled, and went back to sleep.

Erma Bombeck would have approved.

Holding on, letting go

My daughter Amy called me from the top of the Empire State Building early this week. She sounded breathless and cold.

"Hi Mom! Guess where I am?" I wanted to ask a hundred questions, but the connection was bad. Before long, Amy cheerfully ended the conversation, leaving me clutching the phone, hungry for more.

Amy at 16 years old is a young senior, having condensed four years of high school into three. Going on a mission trip is a graduation requirement at our small church school. This year, the three seniors, one junior, and two sponsors flew to New York City—where a multinational Mennonite church thrives in the heart of Brooklyn—for a week of training in cross-cultural ministry.

While she is mature for her age, Amy also is tiny and innocent. What were we thinking to send her from our idyllic country setting to the big city, home of the Central Park jogger, the Mafia, Bernard Goetz, Son of Sam, terrorist attacks, and gangs?

I tried not to hover over her in hand-wringing apprehension, limiting my advice instead to occasional calm suggestions such as, "Make sure you never go anywhere alone! I mean it. You stay with the group."

From the time Amy was conceived, my instinct has been to protect her, to keep her close. For us moms, the near and familiar seems safe and the distant and unfamiliar does not.

When our children were smaller, we lived in the "bush" in Northern Ontario. There were plenty of dangers—bears, drowning in the lake, getting lost in the woods, freezing to death—not to mention that the nearest doctor and hospital were hundreds of miles away.

I came to be at peace with all this, took necessary precautions, and felt like we could hardly live in a safer place.

One summer, a family with four children came to visit. We were down by the lake one evening, and the children played on the dock and walked at the edge of the water. The visiting mother was so nervous she could hardly carry on a conversation.

"Be careful! Not so close to the edge! You hang onto your sister, I don't want her to drown! John, do you see what they're doing?"

I thought, Dear me, Woman, relax. They're perfectly safe.

A few weeks later, we took a vacation and went shopping for the first time in about a year. Getting out of the van and heading into a store, I was terrified.

"You get back here! Don't you wander off like that; somebody could grab you, and we'd never see you again. Watch for cars! Matthew, you hang onto Amy's hand. Look both ways before you cross here. If someone tries to kidnap you, you fall to the ground and kick and scream as loud as you can."

Some distance into this yammering, I realized I sounded exactly like the woman at the lake. No doubt, despite her behavior back then, that mother was perfectly calm when she took her children shopping.

Last summer, Amy and her sister Emily took a walk in the woods and ended up near a cow pasture where an angry bull pawed and snorted at them and tried to break down the fence.

No doubt my jaded New York friends would laugh at me and say that an angry bull rattling the fence is far more dangerous than some dreadlocked crack addict with low-slung trousers lurking in the subway.

Amy called me one day. "Mom, you know what you said about these dangerous dreadlocked guys with baggy clothes? Well, we all got on the subway today and this guy with a really baggy sweatshirt and pants got up and offered his seat to Phebe and me."

And she mentioned another day they were lost on the subway and a dreadlocked stranger was really nice and gave them directions.

Oh.

Amy's almost-daily reports were perky and enthusiastic. She loved her classes, she was meeting lots of nice people, she had a very interesting conversation with a Jewish woman.

"Mom, New York is not dangerous," she assured me one day. "At least in this section of town. We girls walk outside at night."

"Alone?" I yelped.

"Well, the three of us stay together."

That was a relief—sort of.

Amy was doing fine, I had to admit. Sensible and level-headed and well-supervised, she was ready for this. The problem was, I wasn't.

"You have to let them go," another mom told me recently, "if you want them to come back."

Intellectually, I have known this all along. But this time, with my daughter traveling across the country, it was painful and difficult. It meant deliberately going against the primal instinct of all these years to keep her close by, safe, right beside me.

The group flew to Seattle and spent the night driving back home. I was sitting on the couch with my Bible and a cup of coffee in hand early on a Wednesday morning when the front door opened and a small and very pale, ghostly figure glided in, weighed down with a suitcase and backpack.

I enfolded Amy in a hug, laid her on the couch, and dashed off to bring ibuprofen for her headache, a glass of water, and two slices of toasted homemade bread with lots of real butter. This was pure, exploding joy: to have Amy home and to serve her like this. My chick was back in the nest and all was well.

Thankfully, this trip to New York was only a brief flutter from the nest, and Amy isn't leaving for good—yet.

Now, she is busy finishing her courses and planning for graduation. She talks about what she wants to do next year—maybe get a job as a nanny. After that, college; someday she wants to travel or live overseas.

The future is calling my daughter and she's eager to meet it. My job as her mom is to walk this delicate line of holding on and of letting go, of protecting her and of releasing her into the dangerous world out there to find her own path, her own life, a place she finds familiar and safe.

Grace without limits

Our middle daughter Emily was baptized last week. Our family sat on the front pew that Sunday, a fine vantage point for observing the three candidates—15-year-old Emily, her friend Stephanie, and an older girl Phebe. They sat on chairs directly in front of us, looking deceptively serene and almost grown up as they listened to the sermon, the story of Jesus baptized by John the Baptist.

We Mennonites practice believer's, as opposed to infant's, baptism. It is a symbol, a public way to acknowledge a personal decision to follow Jesus Christ. For young people growing up in the church, it means that their pilgrimage of faith is now their own rather than an extension of their parents'.

Baptism requires a measure of maturity, since young people are then expected to be responsible for their choices and to contribute to the work of the church. In the weeks leading up to that Sunday, Stephanie's mother and I wondered if our daughters were really ready for this. It wasn't that I doubted Emily's faith. She has been tuned to spiritual things ever since she was small. If I couldn't answer her questions, she repeated them as though I was half deaf and not too bright.

"Does God have blue eyes or brown eyes?" she asked me at age four.

"I don't know," I said. "See, the Bible says that God is a spirit and ...." She heaved a sigh.

"Mom! Does! God! Have! Blue! Eyes! Or! Brown! Eyes?"

"Blue eyes," I said, figuring that God understood.

At age seven, she made a Valentine's card for Jesus, telling him how much she loved him. She opened the upstairs window and tossed it in the air, certain that he would catch and read it.

More recently, she got a study Bible for teens and read it daily, finding answers to her questions. For instance, she found that God's eyes are neither blue nor brown: "I read in Revelation that he has eyes of fire," she told me. On her own, she found verses to fit her life—on friendship, forgiveness, love, and much more.

While I felt Emily's faith was solid, her maturity was another matter. She seemed much too young for this level of responsibility.

Riding in the van that morning, Emily gave a far different impression than she did sitting erect in her chair at church. Then, she had munched an apple, since she had gotten up too late for breakfast, and rhapsodized dramatically about her new dress that turned out exactly how she had pictured: "This silllllky bluuuuue with sweeping Grecian sleeves." She tossed her head and swept a hand through the air.

I especially had misgivings after the birthday party a few weeks before. This year, Emily chose to spend an afternoon going to garage sales with three friends. As the driver and chaperone, I got an eye-opening insight into Emily and Stephanie's capacity for silliness.

As we drove around town on that hot afternoon, the girls had a staring contest, shrieked about bugs, insulted each others' handwriting and long fingernails, and pinched one another in revenge. Then, seeing horses in a pasture, they instantly dropped the nastiness and, all in unison, burst into a chant: "Four. White. Horses. Standingbyariver."

Descending in a flutter on one garage sale after another, they noisily admired old gloves, fur collars, and anything impractical. A cute little swivel chair with a wrought-iron back brought a brief argument and silent glares until one of them finally said the other could have it.

Stephanie began a story on Belt Line Road and said "like" 14 times before we reached Highway 99. Then, abruptly, she yelled in my ear as a Willamette Ag truck passed. "Kurt! Hey Kurt!"

"Who's that?" the others asked.

"Kurt. He works with my dad."

"Him? He's old!"

"He has some cute kids, like, boys."

By the end of that exhausting day, I thought Emily and Stephanie needed about four more years of intense parenting before they were ready to appear in public again, let alone get baptized.

And yet, these same girls stepped up to the microphone that Sunday morning and shared articulate and moving stories of God's call and their choice to follow. "I've had many questions," Emily said, "and God has helped me find answers for them. I'm far from perfect, but God is daily changing me."

Stephanie read a poem about giving her imperfection to God and receiving love and forgiveness in return.

Next came the vows. "Do you believe in one true, eternal, and almighty God, who is the creator and preserver of all visible and invisible things?"

"I do."

"Do you believe in Jesus Christ as the only begotten son of God?"

They did.

"Don't let anyone look down on you because you are young," the Bible says. Who did I think I was to limit God's grace to the mature and proper?

Emily, I reminded myself, is the one who can keep a carload of little kids mesmerized with the story of Rapunzel, and the one who taught summer Bible school and persuaded a squirming bunch of eight-year-olds to put on a well-organized skit of Daniel in the Lions' Den for their parents.

They knelt to be baptized. One minister held a bowl of water; the other dipped up a handful of water and gently poured it on each girl's head.

My job, I decided, was to give Emily and Stephanie permission to be young, to bless and encourage them, to celebrate.

"Arise and walk in newness of life," the pastor said. I imagined angels all around, rejoicing with us.

The mystery
of marriage

Somehow, it all came together in that moment: lovely bride, tall groom, attentive guests, and wiggly flower girl. Candles burning, bridesmaids watching teary-eyed, a holy hush, and the vows—"to have and to hold until death do us part."

"This," said my husband, "is a great mystery."

It was no wonder that Rosie's wedding affected everyone in her large family. My husband's youngest sister, she has always belonged to all of us, freely sharing the drama of her life so we felt like we were up on stage and part of the action.

Rosie kept us updated on her life as she discovered her musical gifts and developed them, first training at Westminster Choir College in New Jersey, then returning to Oregon to teach music.

She also kept us updated on her frustrating love life. Rosie didn't want just anyone, just to have a man in her life. It had to be the right one, for all the right reasons.

As a succession of young men appeared on the scene and then left, Rosie entertained us with vivid descriptions of them.

"Bill" seemed awfully nice, and they dated for a while, but he finally decided he liked her, but not *that* way. Plus, says Rosie, he had self-esteem issues.

"Mark" seemed promising, a wealthy medical student, but he was into feelings. When they visited his uncle in Portland one weekend, he didn't help Rosie carry her luggage into the house because, after all, he didn't feel like it. Rosie didn't figure there was much chance he'd ever feel like helping out with a sick child in the middle of the night, either, so that was the end of Mark.

"Daniel" was resurrected out of Rosie's past and came to Oregon to see her. A nice guy—maybe this would work out. But, no. "He kept trying to be witty," Rosie said afterward, "and I kept saying 'Duh!' in my mind. I didn't want to spend the rest of my life saying 'Duh' in my mind."

We romantic sisters-in-law ached with her disappointments, and we kept hoping she would someday meet someone as special as her brothers.

"Loneliness has been an issue for me in the past year," Rosie wrote, with characteristic honesty, in her 2001 Christmas letter to friends and family. She went on to describe her gradual acceptance of loneliness as a part of her life. "I am still lonely at times, but the heaviness is gone."

And then, suddenly, there was Phil.

Rosie had slept overnight at our house soon after Christmas so she could stay with the younger children while the rest of us went to the airport early the next morning. She sat cross-legged on the bed, typing on her laptop while I did last-minute packing.

"Oh, I should tell you," she said, "I'm going out with a guy tomorrow night. I've never met him, but he's from Albany. Remember Don Smith, the farmer I worked for a couple of summers? This guy is a friend of Don's and Don thought we should meet. We've e-mailed a couple of times. His name is Phil Leichty."

"Ah," I said, and promptly dismissed it from my mind. Two weeks later, I came home from my trip and my children were bouncing with news—"Mom! Aunt Rosie has a boyfriend!"

Now that, I thought, was quick.

We first met Phil when he and Rosie came over for supper the night of the big storm in February. I had to do my observing by candlelight since the power was out, but Phil impressed me as having the same unassuming confidence that my husband has.

Plus, he talked with the children and put them at ease. "Phil is a phish you should keep," I e-mailed Rosie afterward.

She seemed to agree. "Phil just comes through," she told me. "Over and over. We'll be in some new situation and I'll wonder how he'll react, and he just comes through."

Soon, Rosie had a new light in her eyes and her nieces and nephews were talking about marriage.

"Aunt Rosie, I don't need another Uncle Phil," Ben moaned one evening when she stopped in. He already had two, since Paul and I each have a brother named Phil.

"She won't be our Aunt Rosie anymore!" Emily wailed, and decided she didn't like Phil, and never would.

Phil, who learned a few things while working with kids over the years, asked her to write a poem for him. Emily loved him instantly and soon churned out a masterpiece that said, in part: Leichty was a teacher / Leichty was a coach / I was glad he did not think / my aunt was a cockroach.

She also wrote an ABC poem, touching on Phil's mustache and other important details: N is for nose, right over his fuzz / O is for old, Amy knew that he was.

My girls were stuck on Phil's age for a long time. "He's so old," Amy sniffed, with typical teenage emphasis. "I mean, 41. That's like Dad!"

"Aunt Rosie is 29," we reminded the girls. "It's not like she's your age." But they were unconvinced.

A noisy discussion erupted one day: How are we going to distinguish between all these Uncle Phils?

"They all have different last names," I said. "Why bother with fancy nicknames?"

They tried to be polite, but their faces all read "Duh, Mom. How boring." So, they finally decided, it's Uncle Phil Glasses, Uncle Phil Loud-Voice, and Uncle Phil Big-Socks.

Big-Socks? "Yeah, because when Phil and Rosie took us to the coast, he was wearing these big basketball socks. I mean, they were like knee-socks."

"Over-the-knee socks!" Ben added.

I thought, Uncle Phil Big-Socks. Please.

They announced their engagement in March. Rosie was immediately swept into a whirl of planning and shopping, and, true to form, she swept the rest of us with her.

Our three-year-old Jenny was to be a flower girl, dressed in a miniature version of the bride's dress. Sewing her satin and lace dress was like stitching cotton candy to cobwebs. Whenever I needed to rip out a seam, it felt like the whole thing was disintegrating.

Jenny, sensing my busyness and distraction, grew increasingly naughty. She would sneak out of bed at naptime and squeeze Blistex onto a pillow or shake a thick layer of baby powder on the windowsill.

"Jenny, why do you do this?" I wailed one day. She smiled sweetly, turning on all her Aunt-Rosie/get-out-of-trouble charm. "Cuz I'm a little kid!"

In the weeks before the wedding, I nagged my procrastinating husband about preparing that wedding sermon. "Sermonette!" Amy always added. "Remember, Dad, no more than 15 minutes!"

Paul would pop into the house and find me frantically hemming up dresses, cleaning the house, or mixing potato salad. "Does it have to be this much hassle?" he kept asking. "I mean, we have three daughters. Are we going to have to go through this three times?"

Before we knew it, we found ourselves crowded into the church nursery while a stream of guests flowed into the sanctuary. Zelma the seamstress adjusted bridesmaid dresses and finally resorted to holding the necklines in place with double-sided tape. Jenny kept trying to yank the wreath of roses off her head. In desperation, I grabbed a needle and thread and literally sewed it to her hair.

Then, miraculously, it all came together. Jenny floated up the aisle at the right moment, looking far too angelic to ever dream of rubbing hand lotion into her mother's best quilt. Paul delivered a well-prepared sermon in spite of all my worries, and stayed well under 15 minutes.

"Marriage is a mystery," he said, quoting from Ephesians. "God designed it, and we know it works, but we really don't know how.

"You'd think we'd have everything figured out after 18 years," he went on. "God has blessed me with a wife who is committed to making our marriage work, but we are still discovering the mysteries of love and sacrifice and commitment and how they make a relationship work."

Afterward, we divided up dozens of sandwich buns and gallons of leftover potato salad. Paul was on his hands and knees with a can of WD-40, trying to get sticky residue off the floor where someone had taped down the cord leading to the punch fountain. Someone asked Jenny if she was the flower girl and she said, "No, I was a princess!"

This is the beauty of marriage, and the mystery—that even though two people are happy and successful, they are somehow incomplete without each other. That their joy becomes ours as well. That after 18 years of marriage, my husband can slip a compliment to his wife into a wedding sermon.

And that when I see him scrubbing the floor in his brand-new suit, I can fall in love with him all over again.

"Too busy for you"

No one knows why my husband's grandfather built his grass-seed warehouse on the other side of Muddy Creek when he had plenty of land on this side.

One theory is that he was copying his brother Herman, who had built his warehouse across the creek a few years before. My husband Paul runs the warehouse now, and Paul's brother Steve owns a pellet mill nearby. Both of them are tired of the bridge over the creek.

A concrete slab 30 feet long and 15 feet wide, the bridge might be adequate if visibility were good on both sides of it. While there's a straight stretch on the north side, the south side involves a tight squeeze between the old barn and another building, then a sharp angle, down and left, then the bridge.

More than one piece of equipment has ended up in the creek, and many of us have had the terrifying experience of finding ourselves nose to nose with a seed truck just as we crossed the bridge.

In my case, I had a minivan with four children in it, hurrying home to make supper. Just as I came to the bridge, Uncle James in his ancient seed truck appeared on the other side. I slammed on the brakes and felt the back of the van sliding sideways on the bridge, which of course had no rail of any kind. James's brakes were a bit uncertain, I found out later, but we managed to stop with our radiators about three feet apart.

So I was delighted to hear that they were putting in a new bridge. Nice and wide, guardrails, coming in straight from the road.

The only reason I took time to go watch the process was that my mother-in-law called and asked me to take a message to her husband, who was at the site. When I got there, two men were attaching cables to a tall tree leaning out over the creek, hoping, I was told, to guide it onto the creek bank as it fell.

Part of me wanted to protest, to keep this beautiful tree from being cut down. But then I thought of the new bridge, the convenience for everyone, the vast improvement in safety.

Watching the loggers added to the feeling I've had, lately, that there's something I'm supposed to learn. There is a parallel between the trees in my life and my constant busyness: Sometimes, a good thing needs to go in order to make room for something better.

I love trees. While I am too busy to be a Julia "Butterfly" Hill and sit in a tree for two years to protect it, I am fiercely protective of the trees in my care. I love their stability and grace, their shade in summer and their bare branches against an evening sky in winter.

Except for one huge oak tree, the trees around our house are still adolescents, and I am a long way from my dream of having a house nestled among towering trees like a duck's nest in tall grass.

So I react with mother-hen protectiveness whenever anything threatens my trees. I protest noisily when the county sends a postcard telling us that they're going to trim the branches overhanging the road, or when my husband wants to trim the limb of the walnut tree that's scraping the roof on the back porch.

During a fierce winter storm, I stood at the window and watched the oak tree as the branches bobbed in the wind and even the massive trunk seemed to bend and sway. Silently, I begged it not to fall.

Ever since we moved into this house, my husband had been telling me we should get rid of the two pear trees by the back fence. "No," I said. "Let's keep them. They're trees, and we need trees. Plus, they're fruit trees."

He also wanted to get rid of the anemic maple tree. "Somebody dug it out of the woods and planted it here," he said. "It wasn't particularly healthy to start with, and then someone gashed it with the lawn mower and it's had this big scar ever since."

"It'll be okay," I insisted. "Think of how long it would take another tree to grow this tall."

For some reason, I am often just as protective of my obligations and possessions, all the things that conspire to keep me frantically busy.

"Yes," I say, "I'll take your extra apples. And that bag of plums? Sure, why not?"

"Yes, I think I could teach Sunday school."

"They need boys' pajamas at the Eugene Mission? Maybe I could sew some for them."

"Well…yes, I think we could manage a table at the farmers' market."

"A writers' conference? Sure, I'll go with you."

"Oh, look!" I say, admiring a garage-sale bargain. "This huge piece of fabric for only a dollar, and a rubber stamp for only 50 cents!" I bring them home and they become another obligation, something to store, organize, and use.

Before I know it, I am too busy, with too many commitments and too many things, in addition to the daunting job of running a household.

My three-year-old daughter Jenny learned a Veggie-Tales song this summer. She has a way of singing it when I am at my busiest, like an innocent little prophetess calling me to repentance.

"Busy...busy...," she sings. "Frightfully busy. You won't believe what I have to do."

Describes me exactly, I think.

"Busy, busy, shockingly busy. Much, much too busy for you."

And I flinch. This is the peril of being too busy: Meeting a deadline becomes more important than playing with Jenny, and letting the tomatoes spoil seems like a greater sin than failing to visit Uncle Milford after his surgery.

I was digging iris bulbs beside the house several days ago. I wanted to rescue them before my husband builds a new porch there, and I also thought they might sell at the farmers' market in Harrisburg. As I yanked away a handful of leaves, I found a delicate little oak tree growing among the matted irises.

This is how the obligations come into my life, I decided, like an acorn sprouting silently in the iris bed, small and innocent. But cutting things out of my schedule is another matter, like removing a full-grown oak, involving heavy equipment and cables and permits from the county.

The trees by the fence that I defended so staunchly turned out to be "winter" pear trees. I found that I didn't like winter pears, and getting rid of hundreds of yellow-jacket-infested pears every fall was a dreadful job. Even then, I couldn't quite bring myself to get rid of those trees, even after I admitted that they were ugly—sort of stubby, with dead branches poking out awkwardly.

One of the pear trees blew over in that winter storm. To my surprise, I was relieved to see it go—enough so that I gave my husband permission to get rid of the other one. Now, instead of tolerating second-rate trees, we can choose—flowers, shrubs, or leaving it bare. Or maybe we'll decide to plant more trees, carefully selected to fit that particular spot.

I gave Paul permission to take out the maple tree and replace it with something stronger and healthier. I'm hoping a new oak tree grows by the creek, maybe over by the old bridge.

And I think I'm ready, finally, to do what it takes to cut some good things out of my schedule to make room for the things that really matter, to hear my daughter singing and to know that this time, I'm not "much, much too busy for you."

Gifts and Gratitude

Apple gratitude

My husband's second cousin Leroy Kropf is our near-est neighbor to the east, right where Muddy Creek and Powerline Road curve to the north. Some years ago, an awk-ward little wedge of Paul's grandpa's land butted up against Leroy's, and Leroy asked if he could plant apple trees on it. Grandpa agreed.

Ever since then, Leroy has shared the bounty of those apple trees with Grandpa's descendants. Every fall, brown paper grass-seed sacks, bulging with apples, appear unan-nounced under the west bins at our warehouse.

Like chickadees to a feeder, we flutter to the warehouse to pick up our share. There are red Priscillas, plump Jonagolds, and best of all, bags and bags of Yellow Delicious apples.

I haul mine home and then, rapturously, choose a large, smooth yellow apple, admiring its perfection and feeling its healthy heft in my hand. And then I pause reverently to say thanks.

You might say there are two approaches to giving thanks. The general: "For health and food, for love and friends, for every gift thy goodness sends...." And then, the specific "my-favorite-things" approach—"Doorbells and sleighbells and schnitzel with noodles."

I lean toward the second. Not that I'm not deeply grate-ful for good health and a warm house and a wonderful family, but what really makes me give heartfelt thanks are those apples.

My children like the apples as well, and take the smaller ones to school in their lunches every day. But they think I'm just a bit weird to rave like I do over a mere apple. That's because they don't remember what it was like to live in Canada and do without.

From 1990 to 1993, my husband Paul and I taught at a school for Native Canadians in an isolated reserve in northwestern Ontario, where the lake was frozen over from October until the end of April, and the groceries at the little Hudson Bay store had to be flown in. Milk cost more than $10 a gallon, and the few fresh fruits and vegetables looked tired and cost a fortune.

So, naturally, we seldom had fresh fruit. Grapes and peaches I could do without, but it was apples that I craved, and the few times when I did manage to get some, I was so protective of them that I went just a bit crazy when my supply was threatened.

One winter day our mission director Eugene was flying in from civilization to see us. I had contacted his wife a few days before to ask if she could send some apples along. Sure enough, he arrived with a bag of Yellow Delicious apples. I was thrilled.

After Paul took Eugene to go visiting in the village, I arranged the apples in a basket in the middle of the table and warned the children that I was going to admire them for a few days before any of us took a single bite, and anyone who ate one of them without asking would be in serious trouble. The rest of the day, I gloated over those beautiful apples and anticipated that first bite.

Paul and Eugene returned that evening. As Eugene walked past the table, he noticed the apples. "Hey, those look good," he said. "You don't mind, do you, Dorcas?" Without giving me a chance to answer, he casually picked one up and took a satisfying bite.

I don't know if I looked as stricken as I felt, and I still don't know how I stayed calm when I desperately wanted to scream and weep and pull on his arm and beg him to spare my apples.

Something worse happened two years later. I forget who brought them that time, but again the apples were flown in and I arranged them in a bowl on the kitchen table.

Traditionally, the Cree don't knock before they come inside, so it wasn't a big surprise when two 11-year-old boys from our street burst in the front door one afternoon.

Laughing, they each grabbed an apple out of the bowl and ran back outside.

Oh well, I thought, trying not to panic. I guess I don't mind sharing. Or maybe they're just teasing me and will bring them back.

I looked out the kitchen window, and there were the boys, smashing my apples. Deliberately, they threw one apple and then the other as hard as they could against a tree, then picked up what remained and threw them again and again until they were obliterated.

I felt something terrible and violent boiling up inside of me. So angry I could hardly breathe, I wanted to go out and strangle those two boys with my bare hands.

Before that I sometimes had trouble believing that I was actually the sinner by nature that the Bible said I was. But that murderous rage over two apples properly humbled me, and I knew I had valued my right to those apples far more than my relationship with the two boys.

The Bible also says that all things can work together for good. My deprivation back then has led to a deep gratitude today and a guarantee that I will never be able to take apples for granted.

I know that apples in themselves can never make me truly happy, but as gifts from God and Leroy, they bring a special bonus of joy.

Today, I can hardly comprehend the lush abundance of these seed sacks, bulging with apples, in my pantries. I have enough to give away, to make into apple crisp, to supply the children's lunches, and to replenish the blue-speckled enamel bowl on the kitchen counter.

I admire the pile of yellow against the sharp blue, and then I select a perfect apple and slowly take that first crisp, juicy, delicious bite.

And I close my eyes in reverent gratitude. Thank you, thank you, and thank you again.

Escapes for Mom

I enjoy my job as a mom—most of the time.

On those overwhelming days when the groceries fill two carts, the preschooler asks a hundred questions, everyone talks to me at once, and the phone rings constantly, I think, like the Psalmist, "Oh, that I had wings like a dove. Then would I fly away and be at rest." Or, less reverently, "One more person yells 'Mom!' and I'm outta here."

Maybe that's why I found a recent library book so intriguing. The main character was a 40-something woman, married to a busy man and ignored by her three teenagers. One summer day, she went on a walk down the beach, and without really thinking it through, she simply walked out of her life and started a new life somewhere else. Of course, she soon took in a stray cat and befriended a motherless child, and after all the necessary epiphanies, she was back with her husband and children.

"Every mother's fantasy," the book jacket said. Yet, while most of us moms share these feelings at times, very few of us ever actually abandon ship.

What keeps me from doing something so extreme, I believe, is that I make sure I take miniature escapes. These little indulgences repair the leaks in my canoe, so to speak, bail out the water, and keep me on course downriver.

The first of these is my daily cup of black tea.

During our years in Canada, like so many British subjects, I became addicted to tea. On winter mornings, as frost clung to the windows and the woodstove popped and ticked,

I brewed a large mug of Red Rose tea and warmed myself from the inside out.

My tastes were refined during our months in Kenya, another former British colony, where bushes growing on lush hillsides are said to produce the most richly-flavored tea in the world.

How downright luxurious, now, to wake up early to a silent house, put the kettle on to boil, and brew a steaming little pot of Kericho Gold imported Kenyan tea. I set it on a napkin-lined tray and whisk it to my sewing room, where I sip tea, read my Bible, and feel like the Queen herself.

All too soon, I hear my younger children pounding downstairs like a herd of migrating wildebeests. Cupboard doors slam, chairs scrape, and soon the first "Mom!" of the day ends my quiet retreat.

Fortified with tea, scripture, and half an hour to myself, I'm ready to face whatever the day brings.

By evening, I am ready to collapse soon after the children go to bed, but every now and then I escape into a good old-fashioned novel and stay up until some dreadful unmotherly hour—even past midnight at times.

Last week, I wandered through L.M. Montgomery's *The Blue Castle*. Curled up on the couch, with the children asleep, I immersed myself in page after uninterrupted page of Valancy's transition from browbeaten old maid to strong, assertive woman. The household slept as I followed her right to the utterly satisfying end of the book.

The next morning I was groggy, of course, back in the real world where one never knows how things will turn out the next minute, much less at the end of the story. But what a fun excursion into a world where everything comes out perfectly.

My favorite escape is an evening with friends.

Our first Girls' Night Out was my friend Sharon's idea. She and I have a running joke that one of these days we really need to get together and have a nervous breakdown. We've both earned one several times over, but neither of us is quite sure how to go about it.

Sharon has the good sense to know that even if life is difficult, you still need to have fun. In fact, the more stress you have, the more humor becomes a necessity rather than a frill.

One day, she asked if I'd be interested in joining her and a few other women at Applebee's restaurant in Springfield.

Would I ever. I was excited all day, and as evening approached, I was downright giddy. After Sharon picked me up, I found out I wasn't the only one. "Today was such a long day," one woman said. "I was so looking forward to this."

Another said, "It felt like a first date, trying to decide what to wear and everything."

Naturally, our children thought we were a bit crazy. My teenage daughter sniffed, "The thing is, you guys make such a big deal out of it. I mean, if it were us, it would be just like, whatever, you'd just call people the day of, and say 'Do you want to go out tonight?'"

The seven of us figured out that all together we had 31 children, 29 of them still at home, as I recall. When you have this many children, you don't just like, whatever, go out tonight.

At Applebee's, we talked nonstop, ate, and laughed. I was sputtering and wiping tears and having a wonderfully therapeutic time when suddenly my glass slipper fell off and I realized it was 10 p.m. How did this happen? We couldn't possibly have been there for more than an hour.

Since then, we make a point of fitting these dinners into our schedules. We need them.

Somehow, among the stories and silliness and long discussions, we all grow stronger, fortified for the demands we face every day.

Today, I still need to trim the petunias, weed the garden, cook supper, keep Steven from climbing the basketball post, listen to Jenny read, keep the kitten off the screen door, and try to convince my teenager that a driver's permit is not an inalienable right unrelated to her current behavior.

But I know that tomorrow morning I can sit down with a hot pot of tea, and that some evening this month I can stay up late with Nicholas Sparks's *A Walk to Remember*. And tonight...ah, tonight, I'm off to Ping's in Albany for another night out with the girls.

Daffodil Queen

Once again, I am the unofficial Daffodil Queen of Powerline Road.

My daffodils are the first in the neighborhood to bloom, and they outdo all others in sheer quantity. They march in a vast army under the grapevines and spread in lavish thousands in Mark Smucker's clover field just across the fence.

This happens with no effort or intention on my part. For completely mysterious reasons, these flowers conspire to make me shine. In my other flower beds, blackberry vines grow among the roses, rhododendron plants turn yellow and refuse to bloom, and petunias turn leggy and brown.

The daffodils, in contrast, burst out of the ground in the middle of winter, form buds with frost on their noses, and explode in yellow profusion by Valentine's Day. Strangely, I get all the credit for this, as though I fertilized in the right proportions and coaxed these flowers to bloom their hearts out. In reality, I did absolutely nothing.

No matter how many daffodils are picked, there are always more to replace them. My house is awash in bouquets the children have picked, and their teacher and grandma have been blessed as well. My friend Rita, whose mission in life is to take care of everyone, picked some one day for her children's teacher, her husband's secretary, and a neighbor. She stopped in the next day for more, and the next, profusely apologizing. "I feel so greedy, but I keep thinking of more people to give them to, and they just cheer people up."

"No, Rita," I insisted over and over. "We have plenty. Take a hundred. You don't even have to ask." Finally, I persuaded her to take a bouquet home for herself.

My mother-in-law popped in for a bucket of daffodils, distributed them to her friends, and came back for more. Rita's friend Emily came by to pick some. "Do you mind? Rita said you have lots."

And still, my daffodil supply is undiminished. If anything, it has increased.

Driving toward Harrisburg the other day, I noticed that the long line of daffodils on the west side of Highway 99 is blooming again. How sweet, I thought, of whoever it was who went to all that work to cheer up this stretch of road.

Later, I found out that those daffodils actually came from our place. When she lived here, my mother-in-law explained, she dug up hundreds of bulbs, put them in buckets and garbage bags, and delivered them to an older gentleman in Harrisburg. He would plant them along the highway, and his goal was to have a line of daffodils from Harrisburg to Halsey, a distance of nine miles. Unfortunately, he died before he accomplished his goal, but I notice that he made it at least halfway, past Cartney Drive. Amazing, this one man's labor of love. And how astonishing that he could take that many of our bulbs and not diminish our supply a bit.

I never appreciated the daffodils' dependability as I did this year, when they proved to our new son that the seasons really do change in Oregon. Steven came from Kenya, where the temperature ranges from warm to hot and the bougainvillea blooms all year long. He arrived in December, when the view was bare and brown, and ice covered the puddles one morning. "Now it's winter," we told him, but it won't always be like this. In the spring, it's much warmer. And see out there where that fence is? There will be lots of flowers blooming there. Really."

Steven always looked skeptical, as though he expected Oregon to remain as cold and drab as when he first arrived. But now the daffodils, reliable as sunrise, are proving us right. Steven picks enormous bouquets for me, convinced that if a little is good, more must be much better.

There is a bit of the divine in daffodils, I believe, of grace to the undeserving, of love that multiplies when it is given away, of dependability one can count on, and even a touch of the miraculous.

Back in our first year of marriage, before children and the clarified priorities that come with them, I found Paul to be a kind and affectionate husband with one unacceptable flaw: he never brought me flowers.

I compared him to my friends' husbands who regularly bought roses. I hinted, of course, not yet realizing that hinting to a Smucker was like poking an elephant with a twig. And one lovely spring day after Paul left for work, I sat down and cried.

Realizing that God does not approve when we fail to appreciate his gifts, I called to mind all the things Paul did that I liked, from washing dishes to encouraging my interests to taking care of our finances.

There at the table, I made a vow to God and myself that I would never again hint or nag about flowers. If Paul never brought me flowers for the rest of my life, I would love him anyhow without resentment.

The rest of the day I felt, simultaneously, the terror of great risk and a deep sense of peace.

Then, the unbelievable. Paul came home from work that day and presented me with a bouquet of daffodils. Stunned, I hardly heard him as he explained that he had stopped in at Strubhars to buy fresh milk as he did every week, and Maxine had such a nice bed of daffodils in her yard, so he asked if he could pick some for me since I like flowers so much.

Twenty years later, I still feel the awe of being part of a miracle. Every spring, when I am again transformed from a busy, blue-aproned housewife to Daffodil Queen of the neighborhood, I catch another glimpse of grace and glory and God.

The perfect porch

The city of Kisumu, Kenya, where we lived for almost four months, was hot, crowded, noisy, and dusty. Combined with the culture shock of a Third-World country, it was a stressful place to live.

"You need to go to Rondo," the other Americans kept telling us, with a dreamy, almost reverent, look in their eyes.

So, one weekend, we did, driving an hour and a half to the Kakamega rain forest. We turned off the highway onto a one-lane dirt road, where the forest closed in above us, tangled bushes brushed against the car, and skunk-colored monkeys hopped across the road.

After nine miles, a sign appeared indicating the Rondo Retreat Center. The gates opened and we entered a lovely enclave of green lawns, scattered cottages, and ravishing flower beds, all surrounded by the enormous trees of the rain forest.

My husband checked in at the office and we were escorted to our cottage, a quiet, yellow, wood-sided house, so different from the endless concrete buildings of Kisumu. Our rooms were decorated in the dark, understated style of colonial British days and, best of all, a long, low porch ran the length of one side of the cottage.

We set our luggage in our room and then, while the children set off to explore, I felt drawn to the porch, where I settled into a comfortable wicker chair and absorbed the wonder of that place—the cool air, the quiet, the green beauty. Monkeys scampered through the treetops as though I had personally ordered them for my entertainment, and the stresses of Kisumu seemed a million miles away.

Then, to add the final touch of perfection, a black-vested waiter came up the brick walk with a large wooden tray in his hands, which he set on the little table in front of me. I assured him that he didn't need to serve us, so he left, and I rapturously poured tea from an elegant pot into sturdy white teacups. Then, settling back in my chair with my tea and a piece of cake, I informed my family that I had officially died and gone to heaven.

The exquisite aura of that moment on the porch at Rondo has stayed with me, and I hope to duplicate it in my new porch here in Oregon.

Every house needs a proper porch, I believe, a special place not quite inside and not wholly outside either, yet more than a transition between the two. A destination in itself, a retreat.

We had a porch like that when I was a small child. An old church pew took up one end, a metal lawn chair sat at the other, and morning-glories twined up the posts. We shelled bushels of peas in its shade and snapped green beans by the hour, our add-a-paragraph stories getting sillier as the beans in the bucket diminished. When our work was done, my sisters and I played on the porch, dressing up the cats in dolls' clothes and collapsing in laughter when a kitten tired of our games and took off for the barn with a sunbonnet tied under its chin and a fluffy pink skirt bobbing up and down.

Back then, the front porch was where we met the outside world and talked with people we didn't know well enough to invite inside. The Watkins salesman, for example, would sit there to show us his products, cracking English jokes that I comprehended only enough to be embarrassed. It was also a place for other Amish women to sit and visit with

Mom in Pennsylvania German while we children played in the yard.

Through nearly 20 years of marriage and 10 different houses, I have wanted a porch. A real, old-fashioned front porch, painted white, with hanging ferns and comfortable chairs. Not a deck—too modern. But with a nice sturdy rail, to avoid the carport look.

Instead, I have had a series of small structures with ragged-edged plywood or peeling two-by-six floors. True, they served well their purpose as transitions from outside to in—the children thumped across them hundreds of times and Jehovah's Witnesses knocking at my door found a bit of shelter under the roof. But I always hoped that someday I would have a real porch.

We bought my in-laws' house in 2000, and like all the other houses of my married life, it had a small, fraying-at-the-edges entry. "Someday," my husband promised, "you'll have your porch." So I merrily planned and designed. I wanted the porch to look like it was built in 1911 like the rest of the house and not added on 90 years later, so I took photographs of other houses from that era and studied the porch posts and roof lines. I sketched pictures of the old porches in Ohio villages when we went East one summer, and on the long drive home I planned my perfect porch.

It would wrap around two sides of the house, I decided, east and south, from the main living-room entrance at the front to the kitchen on the south side, where we would replace the windows with sliding patio doors. The posts would taper and the rail would be a small wall about two feet high, solid and authentic.

And then I waited. A new bathroom took higher priority, and then business expenses, and later a trip overseas.

I kept the sketches and my husband frowned as he figured our finances.

Finally, over a year ago, Paul announced that when we rerouted the driveway we would also begin the porch. I was delighted—less so when I came home and discovered the front yard torn up with World-War-I style trenches, and more so when the foundation was built and the floor of the porch began to take shape.

"Now, when is the roof getting built?" I asked impatiently when the floor was done.

"The roof?" Paul said cheerfully. "I told you, didn't I? We can't build the roof till next year."

He had probably told me, but I hadn't wanted to hear it. So I kept waiting, grousing now and then that this roofless porch was worse than no porch at all, like a sidewalk turning the corner and going nowhere.

We went to Kenya then, and Paul arranged for his carpenter nephew to build the porch roof while we were gone. Meanwhile, near Lake Victoria we found a man who gathered reeds from the shore and wove beautiful wicker furniture just like the chairs I had admired at Rondo. "British Airways lets you take furniture as luggage, since it's a souvenir," someone told us. Sensing that my wait was almost over and I was getting even more than I had hoped for, I bought two tables and six chairs for my new porch halfway across the world.

Sure enough, the roof was in place when we came home. It was perfect—hipped at the ends, just as I had ordered it, and it balanced the look of our boxy house, just as I had planned.

The rail is still being built and the posts aren't finished, but I have my porch at last. Sometimes, on warm days, I sip tea in my wicker chair, its curving arms encircling me protectively. The Huns may be invading in the form of nesting starlings in the rafters, and upstairs it sounds like the peasants are revolting, but I am a queen on my regal throne, serenely surveying my kingdom.

"Hope deferred makes the heart sick," the Bible says, "but a longing fulfilled is a tree of life." This is my tree, and I hope to sit in its shade for many years to come.

The best gifts

Gift certificates for our warehouse employees, miniature flashlights on key chains for my Sunday school boys, maybe a new hot water bottle for my mom. My Christmas list has more than 60 people on it this year, and I am deep into the fun but exhausting job of choosing gifts for them all.

While I want the gifts to be appropriate and useful, I also hope I am giving another kind of gift—a present as special as the one I received years ago from two unlikely people.

Looking at him, no one would have guessed that my Uncle Ervin liked pretty dishes. A large, burly man, with a voice somewhere between a raven's caw and a hacksaw, he operated heavy equipment for the city of Hartville, Ohio. It was said that when he drove the snowplow down the street, mailboxes popped off one by one like a child pulling off dandelion heads and tossing them aside.

That may have been because Ervin had only one eye, having lost the other one when a horse kicked him. He enjoyed removing his glass eye and false teeth to terrify the little cousins.

And yet, for all his unrefined ways, Ervin liked pretty things, especially glass. Every couple of years, when we gathered at Aunt Vina's in Iowa, we knew that at some point, Ervin would show up with three white boxes, stiff and new, for me and my two sisters.

Inside, hidden under layers of rustly white tissue paper, we would find something delicate and beautiful. One year, it was milk-glass goblets. Another, little blue glass Cinderella slippers. Once he gave us all miniature china teacups, and another year it was "real" teacups and saucers, made in England, fine bone china.

The teacup and saucer set was given to me during those awful, awkward, adolescent years. The set is on a shelf in my kitchen, reminding me of the other gift Ervin gave me, something much more valuable.

Back then, I felt like I was a nuisance to my older brothers and a frustration to Mom and Dad. My older sister despaired of ever teaching me any social graces.

I think my family loved me, and I loved them. But our relationships were complicated and tangled. Ervin, on the other hand, with the closeness of an uncle and the distance of Ohio, loved me simply because I was his niece. He never mentioned my behavior or analyzed my attitudes.

Instead, he gave me beautiful, delicate glass as though he believed that I, too, were beautiful, delicate, and special. When I dust the teacup he gave me, the gift I remember is the feeling that he loved me for who I was, that I mattered.

Turk Kofstad gave me a similar gift, but in a very different way. I think about him early on Thanksgiving or Christmas morning, when I'm wrestling with the enormous turkey I bought at Safeway. Grunting, I heave the turkey onto the kitchen counter. Then, somewhere between peeling off the plastic wrap and putting the turkey in the oven, I start talking to it.

"Here, Turk, let's pull that neck out of there, and let's tuck that wing under THERE and this one right HERE...and now let's see if there's room for your hind legs right there...."

Talking to Turk the turkey always makes me think of Turk Kofstad, so I turn to whatever child happens to be in the kitchen: "Did I ever tell you I went to school with a guy named Turk?"

"No. What about him?"

"Well, he was a grade ahead of me, and his name was actually David, but he lived on a big turkey farm north of town, so they called him Turk."

"What was he like?"

A good question. Turk was not the kind of guy you reminisce about 20 years later. "He was nice," I say. "Friendly. And funny."

"Did you have a crush on him?" my daughter asked me once. A crush? It never occurred to me to have a crush on Turk. He was neither cool nor cute (today's criteria, my daughter says).

Instead, he was skinny and his teeth were crooked, and he wasn't athletic. But he always seemed to be grinning about something.

Our small-town high school in Minnesota was innocent and benign in many ways. But, as in any high school, it was difficult to be different. Among hundreds of Lutherans in blue jeans, I was an Amish girl in dresses. The kids were kind, for the most part, but I felt like a nun among them, treated with respect but never quite included, never quite acknowledged as a person.

Chemistry class was serious enough whenever Mr. Torgerson was lecturing, but when we went to our lab stations at the back of the room, the class turned into a mad-scientist atmosphere of protective goggles, strange mixtures bubbling in test tubes, and teenage craziness.

I was respectfully asked for help with formulas, but I was not included when people fried all kinds of objects, such as flies, that were never meant to be heated over Bunsen burners.

Turk was in my chemistry class, and one day he held a key in a pair of tongs and heated it above a Bunsen burner. Then, impulsively, he turned and tossed the key onto my chemistry workbook. I shrieked as the key immediately burned down through about 30 pages.

Turk laughed, I laughed, everyone laughed. For the next few weeks, every time I handed in a paper with a key-shaped hole at the bottom, I relived that warm sense of being included, that brief episode when I didn't feel different.

And on Christmas morning, preparing the turkey, I remember the gift Turk gave me of treating me like I was a real person.

At this time of year, gift certificates and hot water bottles serve as visible tokens of my love and gratitude, but the gift I want to give all year long is much more important.

I picture one of my chubby Sunday school boys 10 years from now, tall and rangy and packing to leave for college. In the back of a drawer, he finds a little flashlight on a key chain. If he remembers where it came from, I hope he can also remember the kind of gift I received from Uncle Ervin and Turk: of feeling special, loved, and included, like someone who really mattered.

Mice and the power of nature

This is nothing like living through a hurricane, I know, but out here in grass-seed country we are getting our own little taste of nature out of control. Only afterward do I think philosophically like this, not while I am crawling around my sewing room with a flashlight in hand, having a desperate conversation with an unseen mouse.

Me: Where is that trap? I know I set it right here. Really, I did.

Mouse: No, you didn't. You're all mixed up. Beginning of Alzheimer's, you know. Bwa-ha-ha-ha-haaaaa!

Me: Listen, I know good and well I set that trap right there. At least I think I did.

This is the second time in two days I've been through this. I clutch my skirt around my knees and survey the room, then get down on the floor and cautiously look in the corners.

Then I spy it, under the ironing board one day and behind a basket the next—a floundering, squeaking mouse dragging a gray plastic trap.

"AAAAAAHHHHHHHH there it is! MATT! Where are you?" Matt is my oldest son and frequent rescuer, but he's not at home.

I call my husband with shaking hands. "Paul? C-c-c-can you p-p-please come home ss-s-oon?"

I can't take much more of this.

Normally, I am not squeamish about unwanted animals, having lived in the country most of my life. I have dealt with a bear in the backyard, skunks under the house, raccoons in the corn, nutria in the tomatoes, rabbits in the lettuce, birds in the chimney, bats in the attic, and a squirrel on my kitchen counter. I swat flies with precision and smack spiders with my bare hands.

Here in the Willamette Valley, mice have always been a fact of life. They raise families in the grass fields and run away when the combines come through.

After harvest, I hear mice skittering away in the dry ditches every few steps when I walk down Substation Drive. When the rain begins, they move indoors and we fight to keep them out of the pantry all winter.

Living in old farmhouses for the past 10 years, I have encountered hundreds of mice. I don't enjoy this, but the only time I actually lost my composure was the morning I was pouring Cheerios into my bowl and a fat gray mouse dropped out of the box, scampered out of the bowl, and disappeared behind the peanut butter.

My 12-year-old son was impressed. "Wow, Mom, I didn't know you could scream that loud."

But none of us have ever seen anything like this year—the unbelievable numbers, like a biblical plague.

Most winters, the cold weather inhibits reproduction and the rain drowns out the nests. But a dry, mild winter last year encouraged the mice to proliferate in astonishing numbers.

In the spring, our farmer friend Larry first noticed patches of grass grazed down. By June, we heard reports from alarmed growers of large areas of dead grass, of decimated fields, and of grass moving eerily as hundreds of mice moved through.

Harvest brought more stories. In some annual ryegrass fields, the yields were down as much as 75 percent. Loose dirt from tunneling mice got mixed with the grass seed and made cleaning difficult.

The mice were everywhere. A man near Albany told us he counted more than 100 road-kill mice from one telephone pole to the next. My friend Anita saw two mice wiggle under her screen door in broad daylight and had to close her garage door to keep the mice from running inside. By the end of harvest, otherwise gentle Mennonite girls were climbing off their combines at the end of the day and nonchalantly stomping on mice with their flip-flops.

Our cats feasted on mice and left half-eaten offerings lying in the carport. My six-year-old daughter heard my jaw clicking as I ate a slice of bread and announced, "Mom, you sound like a cat eating a mouse."

Then, after harvest and long before we got any rain, the mice began moving indoors. I set a trap under the kitchen sink and found a mouse the next morning. My son emptied and reset the trap, and an hour later we had another one.

So it went until midnight, when 15-year-old Emily burst into our bedroom and announced hysterically that a mouse was banging around under the sink.

Ten mice in 24 hours, and then Matt bought a spray can of foam insulation at Hurd's Hardware and Paul sprayed it in all the holes under the sink.

This solved the problem, briefly. But this is no ordinary year and these are no ordinary mice. They tried a new tactic, not only moving into new territory, but also messing with my head and disappearing with the trap until I could no longer trust my own mind.

While I do not take any pleasure in killing mice or in see-ing them suffer, I believe this is a just battle. I don't want them in my house, eating my precious stash of chocolate, nibbling on the potatoes.

I don't want their germs and droppings around my fam-ily. But they're welcome to live outside. I'm not going to put poison in the garden or bother them if they run across the yard.

I once wrote an essay for a New York editor and men-tioned my son emptying a mousetrap. The editor felt like this gory detail was too much for her sensitive city audience. Perhaps New York mice are wise and clean individuals like Tucker Mouse in *The Cricket in Times Square*, who lived in a drainpipe, appreciated classical music, and did not produce 2,000 descendants in his lifetime like Oregon mice.

"We thought we had farming pretty well figured out," says a farmer north of us. "This new growth-regulator spray came out a few years ago and was better than anything we'd ever had. We figured, `Hey, we really know what we're doing.' Then this year we did the same things and got half as much seed. It never occurred to us that nature would throw us a curve and we'd have all this trouble with mice."

When nature has the last word, there's not much you can do. At my house, I pray for better days and am grateful for the people around me who sympathize, empty the mouse-traps, and reassure me that I really did set the trap where I think I did.

Since we seldom have extreme weather here in the valley, maybe it's good for us to be reminded now and then how very little power over nature we actually have.

Help wanted: finder and clucker

A combination of factors led me to take stock of my skills and abilities this last month. There was the self-evaluation that comes naturally with the new year, and my occasional worries about what I would do if, God forbid, something terrible happened to my husband and I had to support the family.

Also, I helped my brother's wife find aptitude tests on the Internet when she wanted to change jobs, which made me wonder about my own aptitudes.

And I turned 40 this past year. According to author Jean Lush, I will soon be beyond the sheer-survival mode of a busy mom, and I need to start planning now for new worlds to conquer.

What I found was that I have a long list of dubious skills that could earn me little admiration and less money. I began to wonder what I would ever put on a resume.

I started by asking my family for ideas, and first on their list was my ability to find things. I have a knack, they said, for finding a homework slip at 8:10 a.m., or a microscopic hand for a Lego guy, or the screw that was lying on top of the furnace yesterday.

My daughter said she's amazed at how many phone numbers I have stored in my head, and my son admires my ability to quote a Bible verse for every occasion.

"The people who sat in darkness have seen a great light," I'll tell him, turning on a lamp when he's reading in eye-straining semi-darkness.

I also know every word to every verse of dozens, maybe hundreds, of hymns. My children would find this more impressive if I didn't try to sing them all. "But tim'rous mortals start and shrink, to cross the narrow sea...," I warble.

Recently, I bought two recorders, hoping my home-schooled daughter and I could learn to play together. My kids immediately started picking out tunes.

"Hey, there's do-re-mi-fa-so," my daughter said. "Do you hear that, Mom?"

No, I didn't hear it. I do try to sing in church, although I lip-sync when sitting beside my operatic sister-in-law so she won't hear me, and also because I like to pretend that those beautiful sounds come from me.

At least I'm not like my brother, who refuses to join in the singing at all. "Why don't you just pretend?" I asked him once.

"I used to," he said, "until I realized that I was obviously inhaling while I was supposedly singing."

I'm sure I have no future in athletics or law, as I am terrible at sports, strategy, and logic. I refuse to play basketball, chess, or the mind games my teenagers try on me.

My husband learned years ago that I don't think well on my feet and that we are all happier if he doesn't take advantage of it. We had dated for less than a year when at lunch one day I asked him, "Why don't you eat your broccoli stems?"

"Why should I?" he shot back. "Do you eat tree trunks?"

"No, but...," I stammered, thoroughly confused and filled with a vague, bewildering sense that somehow the logic here was all wrong but I couldn't figure out how or why. A quicker person would have snapped, "No, and we don't eat tree leaves either," but I didn't think of that until about two days later, after he had apologized and I had decided to keep dating him after all.

The only table game I am good at is Boggle, in which you find words in a tray of letters. This has not been a huge benefit to my life, but it was very satisfying the time I played at a New Year's Eve game-night and thoroughly trounced the guy who bragged that no one ever beat him.

I do well at sewing and baking, but am average, at best, in all the other aspects of housework—cooking, decorating, canning, and so on.

However, I feel I am unusually gifted at imitating. This is fine when I read to my three-year-old and cluck like the hen and moo like the cow.

Unfortunately, I am also good at imitating eccentric speakers, not a good hobby for a minister's wife.

If I were filling out an application, the aptitude page would still be empty. What could I write? "I can do a J-stroke in a canoe." "My friend Frances was amazed at how well I drive a stick shift." "A cashier once complimented me on how fast I can write out a check."

At 20, my lack of skills bothered me. Competitive by nature, I felt compelled to be good at everything, embarrassed about the things I couldn't do, and intimidated by everyone who could. Somehow, I was blind to the fact—more obvious to me now at 40—that no one can do everything, or do everything well.

My husband's Aunt Orpha, for instance, seems like a paragon of domestic virtue. But I found out that she had never quilted in her life until just recently when she took a few stitches in a quilt at her nephew's house.

My mother-in-law, who can easily cook a dinner for 20, hires someone to do her sewing. And my husband, computer whiz and businessman, is a poor speller.

Only recently did I begin to understand that our value does not depend on our abilities. God gives each of us specific talents to use to bless others. The more I accept my own limitations, the more I see how all of our talents can complement each other.

A friend and I put on a baby shower some time ago. She is terrified of speaking in front of people, so she planned the menu and I was in charge of the games. My husband's sisters have taught our children all they know about music. I sew for them occasionally, and my husband gives them advice on buying cars. My husband fixes the computer for me when it freezes up; I edit his important letters.

I have even found that my teenagers, for all their delight in confusing me with their twisted logic, will go to bat for me and supply a snappy answer to a stranger's rude comment when I am too tongue-tied to think of one.

Life is short, and I will never learn to be good at everything. Thankfully, however, I am surrounded by family and friends who, collectively, have all the skills I lack. And even my shaky skills can bless their lives in return.

My husband insists that even if something happened to him, we would still be well provided for, and I wouldn't have to get a job if I didn't want to.

He's probably right, but still, sometimes I wonder if there are any openings out there for someone who can convincingly cluck like a chicken.

Your land, my land

The letters to the editor in *The Register-Guard* were running about 10-to-1 against President George W. Bush and his policies the week I left to speak at a women's retreat in Georgia. At the conference, I stood in the lunch line next to a woman whose close-set eyes looked vaguely familiar. "I hope you don't mind my saying this," I said, "but you look like President Bush."

"No, Ma'am, I don't mind," she said. "I believe that man was chosen and anointed by God."

I love this country.

I never realized how much America meant to me until five years ago, when I visited my sister in the Middle East for two weeks. When the plane landed on American soil again, I was surprised by the intense emotion I felt. It was more than a sense of safety and more than the relief of coming home. It was a deep fondness and gratitude.

Last week, as I hopscotched from Eugene to Greenville, South Carolina, and back again a few days later, this appreciation was renewed. I don't often fly, and I still have a sense of wonder at being up above everything and seeing the vastness and beauty of this nation.

The morning I flew out of Eugene, mist hung over the harvested, plowed grass fields as the mountains slept in the background. In Seattle, huge container ships loaded up at the docks in the harbor. As we prepared to land in Detroit, I looked down on the intriguing juxtaposition of a sprawling city, two Great Lakes, and peaceful Canadian farmland across a narrow strip of water.

Descending in South Carolina, I studied the crops below, bumpy-textured and still a deep green. Corn, maybe, or possibly cotton.

We have much to unite us in this country: identical Taco Bells from coast to coast, a common language, and an attitude of embracing change and improvement. At the same time, we have tremendous variety in food, dialects, and interests.

On the way to Seattle, the flight attendant served us Starbucks coffee. In the kitchen at the conference center in Georgia, a 30-gallon plastic garbage can had a sign on one side: ICE TEA ONLY, and sweet iced tea was ladled out in pitcherfuls at mealtimes.

In South Carolina, a homemade sign on the back of a pickup truck announced, "Dale Earnhardt lives!" A large poster in the Eugene airport advertised a new and improved bicycle.

The accents changed as I crossed the country, from the efficient English of Microsoft employees discussing software, to the drawl of the former Minnesotan who sipped his orange juice and said, "It's a bit tricky to hit yer mouth," when the plane hit turbulence, to the warm accent of the South, where each word is stretched out and savored.

I appreciate the fact that it's okay to love your country, and show it—or not. In Canada, where we lived for eight years, being patriotic was not considered in good taste. I believe it was during the 1993 election when a candidate was asked, "Are you patriotic?" and he answered with a roundabout, "If I were accused of being such, I would not deny it."

Mennonites are a bit like Canadians in their discomfort with flagrant patriotism, believing that their heavenly citizenship takes precedence over any they have here on

Earth. Yet it is biblical to love a place, I believe, judging by the psalm written when the Israelites were in captivity in Babylon and longing for home: "By the rivers of Babylon we sat and wept, when we remembered Zion...If I forget you, O Jerusalem, may my right hand forget its skill."

This affection is not a political loyalty, necessarily, since I don't agree with many government decisions, and the affairs of politics are like birds that twitter and fly far above my head.

But it is something more solid, grounded in the land itself and in the people who live here, the warm community spirit of sitting on the riverbank in Harrisburg at dusk on the Fourth of July, listening, with a thousand neighbors, to the Knox Brothers singing gospel songs in the gazebo.

My sister's twice-weekly updates from the Middle East the past 10 years have made me appreciate this country more, in much the same way that I appreciate my husband more when women confide in me about their marriages.

Most Americans, I believe, don't comprehend the level of chaos rampant in much of the world. It may be simple things, such as knowing that if you take a package to three different post offices in a foreign town, you will get three different answers as to how much it costs to mail it. Or the constant expectation of bribes to get anything accomplished, from getting a package through customs to getting a license plate for your vehicle.

And, of course, there are much deeper things, disturbing stories of strange disappearances, shadowy crimes in high places, and elections that are rife with corruption. Even the simplest elections turn dirty, my sister sighs. A nurse, she held a clinic in a tiny village and treated the family of a man who was running for mayor. A rival candidate, they said, had poisoned the family's well.

When "Jill" confides in me about her awful, disappointing husband who buys her flowers and does laundry, but he just won't talk about his feelings, I want to introduce her to "Nancy," who has suffered unspeakable abuse in her marriage for 20 years, just to make Jill realize how nice she actually has it.

Similarly, I am troubled by people on every part of the political spectrum who seem to think that this is a terrible country, one step away from completely going to the dogs. While I don't deny them the right to their opinions, I sometimes wish I could put them on a plane and let them live somewhere else for six months or so. Sudan would do nicely, or Myanmar, or a score of other countries.

America is not perfect, yet for all its diverse elements, it works. However frustrated we may be with a current situation, there is always hope for change.

Packages and people and political processes move across the country with amazing efficiency. We are free to think and express whatever we wish about President Bush, and we are blessed to live here.

The kindness of strangers

"Everyone is always so *nice* to you, so polite, like you're a nun or something," my friend Kim used to say. She liked to go shopping with me, she said, just to see all the cashiers being nicer than normal.

"How do they treat you when I'm not around?" I asked her once, a bit skeptically.

"They're curt and rude," she said. "Not like when I'm with you."

Kim may have been correct in her observation that my Mennonite garb makes people respond more politely than normal, but I still encounter plenty of unkind people. Drivers cut me off. The soulless pencil-pusher at the passport office acts disappointed when I have the right documents with me and can actually get a passport.

An acquaintance, Queen of the Subtle Insult, pokes me verbally where it hurts most. Taken off guard by this behavior, I respond with shocked silence. Then I obsess over it, and, three days later, ironing shirts, I finally think of a brilliant comeback, so wise and witty that it would surely have brought the offender to his knees in humble repentance, if I could only have said it at the time.

But thanks to a comment from my daughter, I think there may be a better response.

Accustomed to the freedom of country roads, I don't enjoy driving in Eugene. It was especially stressful the summer day I found myself on West 11th Avenue with a car full of children, in heavy traffic, searching for the place on the left side that tests the gauges on pressure canners.

A couple of wrong turns found me in a parking lot, and there was no way to get to my appliance store without returning to West 11th. Four lanes of endless traffic zipped by as my desperation grew, and I was sure I would never make that left turn safely.

As I waited, I noticed a bike about two blocks away, piloted by one of those grim, lycraed, helmeted, sunglassed, hunched-over bikers, pumping rapidly down the sidewalk, right toward our car, which had its nose across the sidewalk. I sensed it would not be wise to block the biker's way, but it was impossible to pull out into the street. In my rattled and desperate state it didn't occur to me to simply back up the car.

Soon, the biker braked to a stop at my door, blowing a whistle and yelling angrily. He dismounted, walked his bike around the car, stood by my daughter's window, savagely cussed us out, then shook his helmeted head in disgust, mounted his bike, and went on his way.

Stunned, I wanted to burst into tears, leave town, and never come back. But with this traffic, there was no hope of escape until maybe midnight. And then, miraculously, a minivan slowed down, the woman inside smiled and motioned at me to turn, and a gap in the traffic opened up. I slipped out into the street and fled.

From the back seat, my daughter Emily asked, "Okay, Mom, which one are you going to remember—that nice lady or that mean man?"

She knew I was already stewing about how I should have handled the situation. ("We had homemade cookies in here…why didn't I open the window and give him some as a peace offering?") Emily's words brought me up short, and I immediately made a decision. I would deliberately attempt to remember the woman's kindness whenever the memory of that dreadful man popped into my mind. I would not honor his behavior by forgetting hers.

I want to show my appreciation to all the nice people in my past by making sure their deeds are firmly stuck in my memory. Especially, I want to salute a man I encountered at the Department of Motor Vehicles.

My 15-year-old daughter Amy announced one morning that she was finally ready to take the written test for her driver's permit, so after school we hurried in to the DMV, hoping to get there by the 4 p.m. deadline.

We couldn't find a parking spot until I swooped over and nabbed one on the left side of the road. Just as quickly, I realized that this is not the sort of thing one should do right in front of the DMV. So we tried again, and finally rushed in the door a minute before 4 p.m.

We pulled our number from the red machine—32—and glanced around. Twenty-eight was being served, a few people sat waiting—did we have a chance? I hurried to the counter and asked the gentleman behind it if we were on time to take the test. He glanced at the clock, then at my number, then shook his head.

"You have to be at the counter by 4 p.m., and you're what? Number 32? There's no way you'll make it," he said blandly, without the slightest sign of sympathy.

Amy looked crushed as we turned to leave.

We were about 20 feet down the sidewalk when we heard running footsteps behind us and a man's voice calling, "Wait!" We turned around and saw one of the men who had been sitting inside. "I'll trade you!" he said, waving his number. "I'm number 29, and maybe if we trade, you'll still have a chance."

Amazed, we quickly switched numbers and hurried back inside. Number 28 had just finished and we arrived at the counter as the clock hit 4 p.m. Amy passed her test with a 93 percent.

I thanked the man profusely before we left.

"I saw how disappointed your daughter was," he said. "My daughter took her test a few days ago, and I know how much it meant to her, so I wanted to help if I could."

When Amy left the DMV, she had a new permit in her pocket and a triumphant grin on her face.

I guess my friend Kim was right: people really are nice to me. I want to thank them by remembering.

And, if I have a chance, I want to pass their kindness along at a moment when giving up a few minutes of my time can make all the difference to someone else.

Heritage and Hope

Connecting generations

"**D**o you want to call home and see how things are going?" I ask my daughter Amy.

"Sure," she says, and reaches for the phone, then pauses. "Could someone show me how to use this?"

I teach her how to use a rotary dial, and she makes the call. The two of us are at my parents' home in Minnesota for a week's visit. Amy is 14 and almost inseparable from her cousin Janet, who is 15 and lives next door. My parents are in their 80s, and I feel like I am the uncertain link between two generations, as though I am trying to connect a rotary-dial phone and the Internet.

"Who is Tommy Hilfiger?" my mother asks the girls, who are into brand names.

Dad adds, "Is he your boyfriend?"

Amy and Janet double over, laughing, then Janet gives him a short, shouted lesson in fashion, hoisting up her foot to show him the Hilfiger logo on her sock. Dad looks mystified, either because he can't hear or can't comprehend, or both.

"Come on, we need to see Dad's animals," I tell Amy one afternoon, and we head to the barn.

"Ewwww, that smell!" she shrieks when I open the door. I am dumbfounded. Complaining about a barn smell is like fussing because garden dirt is such an ugly brown.

Amy and Janet are confident and talkative, strong in their opinions and finding lots to laugh about. I wonder what Dad thinks. He always valued decorum and country life, saving his harshest criticism for the times my sister and I acted, as he put it, like silly town girls. If Amy and Janet's behavior irritates him, he doesn't let on, but the girls freely let us all know that the dentist-drill squeal from Dad's hearing aids drives them crazy.

For a while, I feel like I am the only link between these disparate generations, constantly trying to explain them to each other. But as the week goes on, I find to my relief that there are many connections between these girls and their grandparents that go far beyond my groping attempts to find common ground between them.

Amy might turn up her nose at the barn smell, but we are all intrigued by the small flock of nervous goats and calm, heavily wooled sheep that wanders the property at will. When Mom steps outside the back door with a bucket of old vegetables from the grocery store, the sheep all come running, and Amy takes photographs from the window as Mom tosses bunches of broccoli at her flock.

Later, one of the sheep finds a five-gallon bucket out by the barn and somehow gets the bucket over its head and can't get it off. Dad and I circle in slowly over the frozen grass as the sheep baas pathetically inside the bucket. Then we perform a dramatic rescue while Mom and the girls cheer us on from the dining-room window.

In addition, we are all bookworms. No matter where we sit down in my parents' house, there's a stack of reading material within reach. And all of us, I notice, have the same tendency to pick up a *National Geographic* or *Reader's Digest* and be lost to the world within seconds.

The night we look at the quilts, I decide that what connects us most is the history we share, the stories that each generation passes to the next. After the dishes are done, we descend to the basement—Mom and I, Amy and Janet.

First we sit on the couch and Mom shows us a stack of pictures almost two inches high. Each one shows a sample of her handiwork.

"This was Matthew's baby quilt, and this one was Jason's. I made this for Rebecca's wedding."

"This was the first quilt I made after our fire," she says, her voice tinged with sadness, remembering. A tragic fire in 1987 destroyed their house, almost all their possessions, 25 quilts-in-progress, and all of Mom's desire to ever make a quilt again.

It was Aunt Vina, Mom's sister, who came to the rescue, driving up from Iowa some weeks later with a new sewing machine, a rotary cutter, and a box of fabric.

"We're going to make a quilt," she told Mom, guiding her, still dazed and shocked from her loss, through the familiar rituals of selecting the colors, spreading out the fabric, cutting, and sewing.

Something that was frozen in my mother slowly thawed, and after that she trusted her instincts again, gathering scraps of fabric, cutting and sewing them. Today, she has this two-inch-high stack of photos documenting her recovery, and her fabric collection spills out of boxes and drawers.

Our family's history has been marked by fires, and the girls seem to understand Grandma's loss. Janet's family also had a house fire, seven years ago, and Amy remembers losing her clothes and favorite doll in a van fire when she was five years old.

Mom hands me another picture and I immediately notice the flaw toward one end of the quilt—a small square is a quarter-turn "off." Mom says, "Would you believe no one noticed the flaw in that quilt until the picture was developed?" And this leads to another story about Aunt Vina.

"She was making a quilt for some rich lady," Mom says, "and when she was almost done, she noticed that one of the squares was turned the wrong way. She didn't know what in the world to do, because it would have been almost impossible to fix. So she finished it, and when the lady came to pick it up, Vina said, 'There's this Amish custom to have one flaw somewhere in the quilt to keep you from being too proud of it. So this quilt has one little mistake in it somewhere.' The woman was all excited. She said, 'Oh, I hope I find it!'"

The girls giggle, and I smile, thinking of the same determined resourcefulness I see so abundant in Amy and Janet. In fact, Amy is here only because all summer and fall she found creative ways to earn money to pay for her own plane ticket.

The last picture is laid aside and it's time to look at the quilts Mom is working on. Racing against glaucoma, Mom is trying to piece a quilt for each of her 16 grandchildren before she loses her eyesight. She disappears into the spare bedroom and returns with a stack of quilts on her arm.

There is ceremony to viewing a quilt, and ritual, like handling the flag at a military funeral. One by one, Mom selects a quilt off the stack and carefully unfolds it. She holds two corners and I hold the other two, and we all admire that sweep of colors and shapes.

There are Grandmother's Fans, Log Cabins, and combinations of the two. One quilt is an Autumn Leaf, and we all gasp in admiration as it unfolds into a scattering of leaves drifting down on a sunny day.

Janet grows a bit impatient with the process and starts unfolding the next quilt while Mom is still folding the last one, a serious no-no in the unwritten rules of viewing quilts.

Will these girls really appreciate their quilts? I wonder. Only Mom knows how much work is invested in each one. I have a pretty good idea, but the girls, I'm afraid, have next to none.

"How do you think we should decide who gets which quilt?" Mom asks. We suggest having each grandchild list three favorites and having someone outside the family decide. Mom still looks worried. "Some of them are nicer than others," she says. "Like this one. It's nothing special, just scraps."

Then, to my vast relief, both Amy and Janet speak up at the same time, saying exactly what they ought to say.

"It doesn't matter, Grandma. They're all pretty. Whatever we get will be special because you made it."

A generation from now, my grandchildren will no doubt think me hopelessly old-fashioned, with an obsolete computer and one of those funny cordless phones from the '90s.

But I am saving up quilt scraps and stories, confident that as long as we love each other, we will somehow find ways to connect.

Lasting memories and a new humility

It wasn't a typical Mennonite memorial service. Less formal, for one thing, with more reminiscing, and we laughed more than usual. But then, as someone pointed out, Don wasn't a typical Mennonite man.

I have no idea what attracted Don to our church 15 years ago, but I like to think that there was a divine plan behind it all. I used to picture God looking down at our church in Brownsville and thinking, Hmmm...a bit too proper, maybe a little too buttoned-up. They need to learn a little more spontaneity, more love, more humility. I think I'll send them, let's see—yes—Don McGarry!

So there he was, a hot-tempered McGarry among placid Kropfs and Smuckers, a World War II veteran among conscientious objectors, and a history buff talking about Joan of Arc among farmers discussing grass seed.

At the memorial service, I tried to put my finger on what it was that made him so exceptional. Why was it that guests visiting at church soon forgot everyone else but remembered Don, even years later?

"I guess Uncle Don never quite grew up," a niece said. I thought of Jesus' words, "Anyone who will not receive the kingdom of God like a little child will never enter it." I think it was this childlike quality that best explains what made him special. Like a child, Don was utterly honest, humble, and loving. He was easily angered, but he never held a grudge, and minutes after an angry outburst, he would be in tears, apologizing.

It was said that a childhood injury had damaged Don's brain. He never quite recovered, and this was his weakness, resulting in black moods, confusion, and a lack of social skills. But it was also his strength, because it meant that he loved us all with a warm exuberance and displayed a refreshingly genuine honesty in everything he said. One minute he could irritate us to death, and the next minute he would say something so profound that we felt, for all our practiced Christianity, that he was the one who really knew what it meant to follow Jesus.

None of us will ever forget how much Don liked to talk. Anyone who was willing to listen heard long monologues whose subjects jumped from Billy Sunday to Don's cats to rambling recitations from the Bible to that awful government inspector who was coming to see Don's house that week. He buttonholed my nine-year-old son in the restroom and railed about that terrible Mexican bologna he bought that tasted like dog meat.

He left long, meandering messages on his friends' answering machines. He dominated Bible studies while the teachers tried, but seldom succeeded, to tactfully cut him off and steer the discussion back to the lesson at hand. When we shared our concerns at prayer meeting, there was no stopping Don as he rumbled on and on, hardly pausing for breath or punctuation.

"Let's pray for Bill Webster, too, that God'll get him off of that dope he's on; he got madder'n a nest of hornets one time; that dope'll do that to ya. And we won't need to pray for Mrs. Reed, the one we was prayin' for, I believe she passed away. And pray for us to keep close to Christ you know and talk about him so people will call us a fanatic. That's what we wanna do, just talk about Jesus. That'll get 'em, won't it? And pray for me that I'll abstain from all appearance of evil with my tongue, that's my greatest enemy."

At prayer meetings, most of us prayed two- to four-minute prayers with all the right phrases and the occasional thee or thou. Not Don. "I pray for Sharon, Lord. She demolished that little car of hers just like I did that little Datsun I used to have. But I wasn't hurt bad, and I sure hope she wasn't either. Thank you that Sharon never got killed in that accident, Lord. And I pray for my neighbor, Lord. He just flies into a spasm you know when I start talkin' about you. But I do see a change in 'im. He's not gettin' worse. You know the Word says the wicked will wax worse and worse."

The children in church cringed whenever Don started praying. Rumor had it that they used to time him and his record was 14 minutes. Just when I would start feeling really annoyed at him, he would break down and cry. "Jesus, I just love you so much. Thank you for dyin' for a sinner like me." And, I would feel, again, like the arrogant Pharisee in the Bible story, who thanked God that he was not like the weeping publican.

The rest of us waited for someone else to speak first when the minister asked if anyone had a "testimony" to share. But Don would bounce to his feet instantly, pushing up his thick glasses. "Yeah, brother, you know, the Lord's just been so good to me and my asthma's doin' so much better, you know, and I just wanna say I'm through with sin and livin' for the devil, but sometimes I think the devil's in my cat Salem, you know, oh, he just goes wild...." A long time later, he would finally wind to a close and sit down.

If Don liked someone, he showed it. He met me in the parking lot after church one Sunday and said, "Hey, Dorcas, your husband can sure preach! He sure don't lack for words, does he? He just goes and goes like a Gatling machine gun, don't he?" It was probably the only time in history that a Mennonite preacher was compared to a Gatling gun, and I will never forget that unique and genuine compliment.

He also loved his houseful of cats and "A Capella Harmony," the young men's quartet from our church that was gaining a measure of fame in the community. "God is sure honoring our quartet!" Don told me one evening.

"He is?" I said.

"Yeah, my cat had four kittens last week! Just like the quartet!" He chuckled, amazed at this coincidence.

"Are you going to name them after the guys?" I asked.

He grinned. "Hey, yeah, maybe I should!"

And that was how Don came to have four cats named Tom, Byran, David, and Konrad.

Don spent lots of time reading his Bible, and often quoted an amazingly appropriate verse for the occasion. But sometimes he read things into scripture that no one else had ever seen. I was helping him scrub his kitchen one day, trying to ease his mind about the HUD inspector coming the next day. When I wiped the coffeepot, Don said, "Do you like coffee?"

"Yeah, I like coffee," I said.

Don laughed. "Well, me, I'm just a surfer when it comes to coffee."

I stared at him. "A surfer?"

He nodded. "You know, the Bible talks about surfeiting and drunkenness, and I don't get drunk no more, but I sure do like coffee, so I guess I'm a surfer with coffee!"

"I...guess...so," I managed as I went back to washing the stove.

They found Don on his living room floor one Sunday morning in April. His exhausted heart and lungs had finally quit altogether.

Since then, I sit in church and glance over at his aisle seat, expecting him to jump to his feet with fresh news about what God has done for him lately. I wait for his rumbling voice at prayer meeting, and it never speaks.

But I sense a subtle change in the rest of us—a new openness, perhaps, and a new humility. Soon after Don's death, my husband Paul asked the congregation, during a Sunday service, if anyone had a testimony to share. Many of us talked about what Don's life had taught us. "I've never seen people get to their feet so quickly and speak so freely," Paul told me afterward.

This, we're learning, is the paradox of God's kingdom— that the least will become the greatest, that the one who humbles himself will be exalted, and that a little child will lead those of us who think we're all grown up.

Seven-foot brothers

*M*y youngest daughter, four-year-old Jenny, likes to jump on our trampoline, but not by herself. "Can you jump with me?" she pleads. But her siblings never want to because they're not allowed to "jump wild," as they put it, because she can't keep her balance.

One day, however, Jenny sweet-talked her oldest brother Matt into jumping with her. I looked out the window and saw, not both of them jumping separately, but six-foot Matt holding three-foot Jenny in his arms, her arms around his neck, her legs wrapped around his waist. Slowly and gently, he bounced her up and down and around the trampoline in a strange and quiet and beautiful dance.

Watching, I prayed: Please, may this always be what she remembers about being his little sister.

When I first came to Oregon, I lived near Halsey with a family who owned a grass-seed warehouse. One evening, I went up to the flat roof of the warehouse, some 40 feet high. Then I climbed up a ladder another 10 feet to the top of a little platform, where I had a great view of the sun setting behind Mary's Peak, and I snapped a few photographs.

When I descended the ladder, I was startled to see the warehouse maintenance man on the roof fixing something. "Good evening," he said. "I'll bet you have three brothers."

"Yes, I do," I said.

"And they're all older than you," he went on.

"That's right," I said. "But how did you know?"

"Just the way you went climbing up there," he said vaguely, chuckling to himself, and that was all the explanation I got.

Upstairs the Peasants are Revolting

Two of my brothers, Marcus and Phil, were at my house overnight recently, here to celebrate our son's graduation from high school. The next morning, we worked our way through three pots of coffee, the newspaper, and a few subtle family jokes. And, as I always do when I'm around them, I pondered my role as their sister.

It is a strange and solemn thing, this dance of big brothers and little sisters. First, we idolize our brothers and then, disillusioned, we turn away. And finally, if we're fortunate, we develop a new and healthier relationship. Years later, we find they have influenced us in ways we never imagined.

As a child, I thought my brothers were like gods: about seven feet tall, all-knowing, utterly confident. I believed everything they told me and did anything they asked me to do. On the night in 1969 when men first landed on the moon, my third brother Fred knelt at the bedroom window, gazed at the full moon, and convinced us all that he saw little black dots moving around on it. My sister and I looked, and sure enough, pretty soon we thought we saw them, too.

He also convinced me that pig feed was good to eat, so I'd often munch on a handful of pig pellets while I was doing chores.

When he told me that the "FD" on the little Fisher-Price fire engine stood for Fatty Dorcas, I believed that, too, and thought I was fat, even when we went to the principal's office in sixth grade for "height and weight" and I weighed only 67 pounds.

When one of my brothers told me to put my hands in front of me and lace my fingers together, I promptly obeyed. He then grabbed my fingers and squeezed them together, a painful experience that, I later read, was sometimes used as a Communist torture.

I believed Phil when he told chilling stories at night back in the days when five of us slept in one room. Cold fingers scratched at the windows as he spoke, the attic door slowly opened, and terrible ghostly forms waited in the closet.

When my brothers repeatedly told me that I was ugly and disgusting, nothing but a crybaby and a tattletale, I was sure they were telling the truth. That was more painful than anything else they did, so much so that it colored all of my memories of that time. When my children were old enough to ask for stories from my childhood, I was unable to remember the good times my brothers and I had shared.

As a child, I tried all kinds of inappropriate ways to get their attention and approval. By the time I was out of high school, I decided that I meant nothing to my brothers, and never would, and it was time to move on and make my own choices whether or not they noticed or approved.

In the strange way that these things work, when I had given up trying, it started happening. An occasional phone call, just to talk; a birthday card; a late-night conversation when the family was together.

I hardly knew how to handle it, some years later, when one of them wanted my opinion on a big decision he was making. "Do whatever you want. It doesn't matter what I think," I told him, repeating the lesson he had taught me so well.

I wondered when this happened—where in our long journey as brother and sister did our paths reverse to such a degree that now he not only wanted to know what I thought, he also wanted my approval?

One day last year, in the middle of a phone call, Fred abruptly asked, "Dorcas, how mean was I to you when we were kids?"

"Um...well...," I stammered, caught off guard and trying to be tactful.

"Okay," Fred said, "I was mean. Really awful. Well, I just want you to know that I'm sorry. I really am. And I apologize, for everything."

I didn't realize how much I had always wanted to hear those words until I heard them, or how much I wanted to say, "I forgive you, I really do, for everything" until I said it, my tears mixing with the words to wash and heal a wound somewhere deep inside that I didn't even know was there.

Fred went on, "I've been doing some thinking and realize that I've believed a lot of lies."

He started me down the road of examining my beliefs as well, what is true and what is false. At Matt's graduation, we took a picture of him with his two uncles. I was startled to see that he is taller than both of them, and I realized that the seven-foot giants of my memory were actually never all that big.

Nor were they very old. The time Fred pushed me, fully clothed, off the dock and into Lake Koronis, he was only about 14 years old. I thought he was almost grown up, but he was just a kid, coping with a difficult adolescence with the only tools he had.

"Phil remembers you as this cute little sister that he was very fond of," his wife told me. This puzzled me, until I remembered that Phil, though he may have been emotionally distant, was actually not unkind. I had unfairly associated the painful memories with all of my brothers.

And I no longer see them as being utterly self-confident. They have normal bouts of self-doubt and regrets.

More and more, I remember the good times. The time I was sick and Marcus bought me a bottle of orange pop, a rare treat. The times Phil taught me English words so I would know more than Pennsylvania German when I went to kindergarten. The times Fred took me exploring in the woods.

My children think I harp endlessly on how their behavior toward each other now will influence their relationships 30 years from now. It is only because I want their memories to be of encouraging words, of good times, of being held in a big brother's arms and gently bounced.

But since they are kids, after all, I also teach them to say those miraculous words of healing and restoration: "I'm really sorry. And I apologize, for everything."

I will never know all the ways my brothers have influenced me, but I like to think that, despite the hard times, I have climbed ladders in life that I would never have attempted if I had not been their little sister.

A patchwork of personalities

It had been 15 years since my five siblings and I were all together, but last month we assembled in Minnesota to celebrate Mom and Dad's 50th anniversary. Two weeks later, my husband's family gathered for three days at a retreat center in the Coast Range.

One would think, at first glance, that these two families are similar. Six siblings in mine, the Yoders; seven in Paul's, the Smuckers. Silent grandpas and indulgent grandmas. Ladies and girls in long skirts or dresses. An Amish/Mennonite heritage with its thrift and hard work and high-carbohydrate food. All of us followers of Jesus Christ. All the children from solid mom-and-dad homes.

However, somewhere among the coffee and conversation, I realized again that these two families are fundamentally different. We used a gallon percolator at the Yoder gathering and brewed coffee twice a day, sometimes using Mom's drip coffeepot in addition, for batches of decaf. At the Smucker reunion, I got up early every morning to make a glass pot of coffee in the restaurant-style coffee machine, but ended up pouring most of it away when, by afternoon, only four or five cups were gone.

My family is creative but not terribly organized, which is why my mother pieced 16 patchwork quilt tops—one for each grandchild—but we didn't know until Saturday morning that she wanted to distribute them that day. My brother's wife and I hung the quilts on the clotheslines, forming a stunning kaleidoscope of colors and shapes and moods rippling in the breeze.

The family assembled, and suddenly Mom had a panicky look on her face. She turned to me.

"How will we decide who gets which one?" she whispered. "Shall we go oldest to youngest?"

"Sure. I mean, I guess so," I said, since no one else seemed to be taking charge. "But let's let the older girls go first, since the guys don't care what they get."

Each of the older grandchildren gathered his or her quilt off the line, and the youngest ones took what was left. While all the quilts were beautiful, some of the colors were less attractive to modern fashion-conscious kids, and these were the last ones chosen. This sent me into a flurry of anguished second-guessing. If only I had known about this ahead of time and done more planning so that everyone could get his or her favorite. But then, I am a true Yoder, given to excessive reflection and regret.

Had this been the Smuckers, the quilt distribution would have been planned with more strategy than a political convention, with each quilt numbered, three ballots for each grandchild, and no time wasted on hindsight.

Grandma Smucker hates to sew, so distributing quilts wasn't an issue. However, every detail of their reunion was organized months in advance through lively e-mail discussions and then finalized in a four-page e-mail from Rosie. Final Reunion Notes: Sunny-Day Schedule, Rainy-Day Schedule, Things to Bring, Duties, Free-Time Activities Available, and Stories and Ideas for Reminiscing Sessions.

The Yoders love language—puns and subtle jokes and mimicry. We remember personalities more than events, and imitate aunts and neighbors from long ago.

When Emily flicked her long ponytail across the kitchen counter, I instantly repeated the German command Mom always told us, literally translated, "Fling not your hair the kitchen around!" The granddaughters tried to repeat it, stumbling over the guttural r's.

We recounted my brother Fred's famous joke about the bank teller named Patty who didn't think she should let a frog borrow money since all he had for collateral was a ceramic swan. Hillary, my niece, figured out the punch line and started giggling 30 seconds before she was told that the manager said—naturally—"It's a knickknack, Patty Wack, give the frog a loan."

Unlike the Yoders, the Smuckers are athletic and competitive, thriving on activity. Tournaments were arranged and posted on the wall at the retreat center: table tennis, horseshoes, and basketball.

Paul played his 11-year-old niece Stephanie in the ping-pong tournament, and barely beat her, which meant that next she would play Uncle Phil. I was in the kitchen a few minutes later when Stephanie's mother Bonnie burst in, laughing.

"You should have seen it!" she hooted. "These two big uncles were discussing how to beat skinny little Stephie. Phil was actually asking Paul what her tricks are, and Paul was warning him that he can't beat her by putting a spin on the ball because the paddles are worn out." Bonnie left, still chuckling, to watch the game.

Stephanie won, 21-17.

We reminisced at both gatherings—spontaneously among the Yoders and at a scheduled time with the Smuckers. The stories gravitated toward past disasters and near-misses: the time Paul nearly chopped off Phil's fingers with a hatchet, the time a snake bit my brother.

The Yoder catastrophes often resulted from our uneasy relationship with motor vehicles, having been Amish for so long that Dad seemed to feel that repairing brakes was optional and you could always pull on the steering wheel and yell, "Whoa!" This resulted in my brother Marcus losing control of a tractor on a steep hillside, and Dad crashing the car into a pump at a gas station.

Most of the Smucker disasters resulted from plunging headlong into danger, a trait that seems to contradict their tendency to plan and organize. There was the time Paul rode his tricycle on the flat bed of his dad's truck and fell off, and the winter night when Phil drove a snowmobile into a field and hit a barbed-wire fence.

At the Yoder gatherings, Paul tends to fade into the background, reading old *Reader's Digest*s while the rest of us forget he's there and lapse into German. With his family, I mostly listen to the hubbub because when I try to say something, no one hears me.

Yet somehow Paul and I, coming from these two disparate families, have formed a combination that works—my bright ideas with his practicality, his aggression with my caution. I drink coffee; he drinks milk. I laugh aloud at James Herriott books. He frowns intently over John Grisham.

Like red and blue combining to make purple, his fiery family background and my contemplative genes have merged in the vivid characters of our five biological children. Our daughters are fearless and creative. Both of our biological sons love sports, and both have also been known to lie awake at night worrying about house fires or cougars prowling along Muddy Creek.

Our kids grow up on Grandma Yoder's stories and Grandma Smucker's potato salad. A few are organized;

the others let life happen as it will. They all know bits of German, but none of them likes coffee.

Each of our children is unique, like a block on Grandma's quilts, distinct and separate, yet blending into the vast and beautiful patchwork of family, a rippling kaleidoscope of color and personality and love.

Fearing the Fatal Error

I always thought my dad had a strange relationship with his vehicles.

He relied on a Farmall M and a John Deere 720 to plow and plant and bale hay, and on a series of large old cars to transport his family. But he never seemed to understand how they worked, and when they broke down, he seemed to take it personally. Mystified and frustrated, he had no clue what to do except haul them to the shop.

To this day, Dad has a tentative, deliberate way of fastening his seat belt, turning the key, and putting the car in reverse, like a new pilot on a solo flight. He avoids freeways, preferring back roads and familiar routes.

I see that same deliberate caution in myself when I use a computer, the same reliance on the machine but with no idea of how it really works. When I venture off the familiar roads of Word documents and Juno e-mail to try something new, I fearfully click here and then over there and sigh with relief when nothing blows up in my face.

In contrast, my children grew up with electronics and seem to have a oneness with them, the keyboard an extension of their hands, the computer somehow connecting directly with their brains. My son grabs the mouse and clicks recklessly—moving this, dragging that, opening something else. Watching him feels like skidding down an icy road at 60 miles per hour.

119

Coping with today's electronic devices helps me understand my parents just a bit better. After a week of aggravation, our computer is working again. Microsoft Word opens when I double-click the little picture and Juno brings messages from my sister and daily decluttering tips from FlyLady.

Such a remarkable machine, so convenient, so efficient—what would I ever do without it? But only last week I thought it was an arrogant invention that refused to listen to me and had no mercy on my desperation. As icons disappeared and Fatal Error messages popped up, I wanted to throw it in the garbage and go back to being Amish.

I know basic first aid in such cases—hit control-alt-delete, restart the computer. Beyond that, I panic, certain that all my files are lost forever.

Thankfully my husband Paul can perform minor computer surgery, even raise the dead at times. While I hover restlessly in the background, wringing my hands and praying, he pops in CDs, pushes buttons, reformats the hard drive, and (oh, the relief) miraculously puts everything right.

At these times, I have a new sympathy for my parents. Computers and cell phones stymie me at age 42, but Mom and Dad were in their 50s when they left the Old Order Amish church and joined the modern world with its cars, tractors, electrical appliances, cameras, and phones.

It seems to me that young minds are wired to understand new technology and older ones are not. Somehow, teenagers understand how things work, why they break down, and how to fix them. They incorporate new inventions into their daily lives and use them as casually as a toothbrush. Past the age of 35 or 40, the mental switches start to turn off, and gadgets and machines become a mystery. We need them, we rely on them daily, but they are impossible to understand and often frustrating beyond belief. Sometimes, we fear them.

My husband is an exception to this rule, but it has proved true for my parents, myself, and my children, each generation embracing the technology of its youth but developing a fearful awe toward the gadgets introduced later in life.

Telephones, for instance. None of my grandparents ever had a phone, and when my parents first got one, it was a jangling affair, with a two-foot cord, right in the middle of the house. Thankfully it didn't break down like the car often did, but Mom and Dad still seemed half afraid of it. They made phone calls ceremoniously, cautiously picking up the receiver and turning the rotary dial. "It's already ringing!" Mom would announce, amazed.

My sisters and I had no trouble learning the art of chatting for hours on the phone, but Dad never has. He is still back in the era when a long-distance call meant that someone had died. "Hello? Dorcas?" he says. "Yes. Well. How are you? Do you want to talk to Mom?"

Unlike my parents, I use the kitchen phone so much some days that it feels attached to my ear. But I am not nearly as blasé about my cell phone, a lovely little device that came into my life a couple of years ago. How convenient—how modern and chic, really—to whip it out of my purse in the bulk foods aisle at WinCo to call home and ask how much cinnamon we have left.

However, I use the cell phone only for basics. My children pick it up in the car and casually punch buttons—saving numbers for me, changing the ring tones and backgrounds, hunting for games. "Now, make sure you get it all back to how it was before," I harp nervously. "I have no idea how to undo what you're doing."

They chuckle. Poor Mom, still half Amish.

Recently, I gained a new understanding of the changes my dad faced when he left the Amish. Over lunch with Dad's brother John a few days ago, my sister asked what my dad was like as a young man.

"Your dad was the best horseman in the county," Uncle John said. "He could take a team of horses and plant the straightest rows of anyone. We all thought he was the expert. Your dad used to say that horses were better than tractors because tractors rounded off the corners of the field and horses made them nice and sharp."

My sister was astonished, and so was I when she told me. We had never heard this before. To think that Dad, so inept and bumbling with anything mechanical, had been the community expert on horses when he was young.

What was it like for Dad, I wonder now, to trade in horses for tractors, to lose expertise to gain efficiency, to see his sons more capable at fixing machinery than he would ever be? We knew Mom and Dad left the Amish because they felt it was best for their family, but we had no idea of what Dad had sacrificed in the process.

I suppose this is how it will always be—the young will be the experts and older folks will struggle with change. I expect that my grandchildren will someday use technology that will completely bewilder my children, and Matt or Amy will call me on their old-fashioned cell phone and tell me that they finally understand.

From baby to bride

hen I left home at 19 to come to Oregon, my parents and two sisters took me to the airport. "The ride home was really quiet," my sister told me later. "Even Dad had tears in his eyes."

Why in the world, I wondered at the time, would anyone be sad, let alone shedding tears, at my going away? Kids are meant to leave home someday, after all, and my parents' lives would be easier and quieter without me.

Life was all future, then. The present was endurance and impatience; what mattered was the next door to open, the next adventure.

Now, on the other side of 40, the present matters most. Some days, I would give almost anything to slow down time and to make things stay exactly as they are. Especially after a month full of travel and change, I understand those teary eyes all too well.

It began with my niece Annette announcing in a gleeful e-mail her engagement to a Lancaster County, Pennsylvania, dairy farmer.

Three weeks before the wedding, my younger sister Margaret, also from Pennsylvania, gave birth to her third child. She would have a houseful of guests over the wedding, so I put my 17-year-old daughter Amy on a plane and sent her ahead of me to help her aunt for two weeks.

My parents are in their 80s, but my siblings and I felt that they needed to be at Annette's wedding. We decided that I would fly to Minnesota, pick them up, and escort them to Pennsylvania.

Upstairs the Peasants are Revolting

It was a strange journey that week, of tears and laughter, of bumping into the past and being pushed into the future, and of the present overlapping with both until it was hard to remember what was now or then or still to be.

Seventeen years ago, my sister Margaret was a petite and cheerful teenager who came to help me when Amy was born. She did my housework, took my two-year-old on walks, and deliberated over which watch and socks to wear with which outfit.

Today, Amy looks remarkably like Margaret did back then, and as Amy washed dishes in Margaret's kitchen, wrestled toddlers in and out of car seats, and wore her fashionable Aeropostale sweatshirts, I had an uncanny sense of the past and present telescoping into one.

At the wedding, I had the same sensation of the past intruding on the present. Annette, the bride, was the baby who first made me an aunt, and my old photo albums are full of pictures of her—posing with the cat, opening Christmas gifts, dressed up in whatever strange costume her three aunts concocted.

As Annette floated up the aisle in a beautiful shimmer of white, my sister and I, through our tears, had a sudden sense of deja vu, of the little niece she used to be, and of an old photo of Annette at four years old, dressed like a bride with an old organdy curtain on her head and silk flowers in her hand, standing in front of a refrigerator box turned into a playhouse, grinning at the camera and her indulgent aunts.

When did this happen? I thought. When did I blink and that day became this one?

It was in my parents, however, that I saw the most pronounced results of time passing.

When I was small, Mom was the one who took care of me, firmly holding my hand to cross the street. Later, she always made sure I locked the car doors before I drove anywhere alone.

When I had small children, she loved to do my laundry and pamper me, knowing the difficulties of babies and sleepless nights.

But this time, I took care of them. At home in their farmhouse, they still seem competent and self-sufficient, but in the vastness of airport terminals they seem small, frail, and lost. Long ago, they took me to the airport and made sure I had my ticket. In a complete and jarring reversal of roles, I drove to the airport, got our boarding passes, and then hovered, worried, and reminded: "Do you need a bathroom?" "Are you hungry?" "Do you have your bag? What about your heart pills?"

To navigate the long distances in Detroit's airport, I put both Mom and Dad in wheelchairs. Seldom have I wanted to reverse time as much as I did then, seeing the parents that were once healthy and hardworking being helplessly pushed along by others.

Two weeks after we came home from Pennsylvania, Amy traveled, all alone, to the United Arab Emirates for a five-month project of teaching the three daughters of an American family.

We watched her as she waited to go through security. Then she looked back at us, grinned, and marched jauntily off to her gate as my husband held me and I cried out the savage pain of letting her go.

When time and change make daughters leave home and parents become older, I want to clutch the present and never let go. And yet, only when the present dissolves into the past can little girls grow up to help others, teenagers find their calling, parents become grandparents, and grandparents see a beloved granddaughter walk up the aisle on her father's arm.

I don't know the sort of life I would have led if my parents had refused to let me go to Oregon. I hope it would have been good and full, but I know I would never have been blessed with this particular life—this husband, this home, this amazing reddish-haired daughter off to welcome a future of her own.

Changes and
a Child

The turkey and the vine

Perhaps our decision to go to Africa can best be explained by two stories, one involving a turkey and the other a vine.

The first story began with a typical Christmas ritual, probably repeated in a million American households. Half a dozen siblings, parents, and in-laws surrounded the island in the kitchen to transfer the turkey from the roaster to the platter.

My friend Liz was among the people gathered around the island as the process began with someone spreading an old newspaper over the counter to catch the drips. As her father-in-law prepared to pull the enormous bird out of the oven, Liz began to read a few paragraphs in the newspaper spread in front of her.

Suddenly, a small news item caught her eye, and she read with a growing sense of horror. A family (possibly Kurds from Iraq; I don't recall) was escaping over the mountains into Turkey. A husband, wife, and three or four children were locked in the back of a truck that was carrying them to, they hoped, a better life. It was bitterly cold, and one by one the children succumbed to hypothermia.

The parents desperately pounded on the walls of the truck and shouted for help, but apparently no one heard them and the truck kept going. By the time they reached their destination and were released, the children were all dead.

"Listen to this!" Liz exclaimed, and read the story aloud.

"Hmmm. Yes. Terrible," the others said. "Now, where's that pot holder? Here, careful with that platter. Hand me a fork, will you?"

"I stood there," Liz told me later, "and I was just overwhelmed with the sorrow of those parents in that story. But I felt like, to the people around me, their suffering had no meaning and no significance except as a little bit of newspaper to catch the drips from the Christmas turkey."

And then, there was the vine. My husband recently wrapped up a series of sermons based on the book of Jonah. We all discovered that this book is much more than a fanciful children's story about a man who was swallowed by a whale.

After Jonah was deposited back on dry land, the Bible says, God gave him a second chance and told him, again, to go to Ninevah to tell the people they were going to be destroyed for their wickedness. Jonah gave his message and then sat on a hill outside the city, waiting expectantly for judgment to fall on these enemies of Israel. As he sat in the hot sun, God made a vine grow to give him shade.

Jonah was grateful for the vine and the benefit it provided. But to his disgust, the people of Ninevah repented and were not destroyed after all. Worse, a worm chewed through the vine and made it wilt, so his shade was gone.

As Jonah sat pouting in the sun, God showed him that he had cared more for a temporary physical comfort than for the lives of thousands of people that God loved as much as he loved Jonah.

This is why we are taking our family to Africa for four months.

Like most Americans, we enjoy our comfortable and insulated lives. Reading a newspaper article about some terrible car-bomb explosion on the other side of the world, we scan the paragraphs to see if any Americans were hurt or killed. If there were not, we unconsciously feel that maybe it wasn't that bad after all, and we are still safe and all is well.

My husband and I have often wondered how, in all of our comfort and affluence, we can give our children an accurate perspective on how blessed they are in relation to most of the world. How do we teach them that their blessings come from God with a responsibility to use them wisely and share with others? And how do we teach them that other cultures have much to teach us, and that every person in the world is as valid and valuable as they are?

The best way, Paul and I decided, would be to show them firsthand.

So, a couple of years ago, we began to pray about a family service project in another country. We wanted something that the whole family could be involved in, in a place that was reasonably stable politically, where English was the main language.

Once we decided that we really wanted to do this, things began falling into place. Paul suddenly had requests for custom work at his grass-seed warehouse, enough to finance the whole project. We found someone who could live in our house, take care of the warehouse, and process orders for my new book.

Our daughter Emily, who had been in poor health for a couple of years, was diagnosed with allergies and gradually regained her health. And through a friend of a friend, we found a place to go: a small organization in Kisumu, Kenya, that takes in orphaned street boys and provides them with a home and an education.

As a former British colony, Kenya fit our language criterion. And, as African countries go, it is quite stable politically. However, like much of Africa, Kenya has been ravaged by AIDS, with roughly one million of its children orphaned by the terrible disease.

Rick and Audrey McAninch, originally from Washington state, started the Into Africa Foundation to work with boys who have been orphaned by AIDS. Girls, they tell us, are more likely to be taken in by the extended family because the women do much of the physical work of the family and also have value as brides. Boys often are turned out into the streets at eight or nine years old.

While we expect to involve the whole family in our work, we still have a somewhat vague picture of what we will actually be doing with the boys and for the organization. We do not have grandiose plans or agendas. We don't plan to change a culture or rescue a thousand orphans. But maybe we can make a small difference in the lives of one or two.

We want to go with a teachable attitude. We would like to get acquainted with the land, people, and cultures of Kenya. We want to learn more about the world and our place in it.

Most of all, I want us to learn the lessons of the turkey and the vine: We are blessed with privileges and comforts such as shopping at well-stocked stores, enjoying a Christmas turkey, and living in the safety of rural Harrisburg.

All of these are wonderful, and we appreciate them. But the lives of people, whether from Oregon, Kenya, or anywhere else, are eternal rather than temporary and infinitely more worthy of our time and resources.

The sound of dignity

*B*ack in Oregon, a train whistle often wakes us up in the morning, or the oil furnace rumbling to life rouses us.

In Kenya, we wake each morning to the sound of swishing brooms. The windows have screens to deter mosquitoes and iron bars to deter thieves, but no glass. So the morning air glides in around the curtains, and the morning noises filter in with it. Roosters crow, dogs whine, children yell, and the brooms swish.

The swishing begins before dawn, before the sun leaps over the edge of Kenya with hot intensity. As I lie in bed, savoring the brief coolness, I can picture Martin, a former street boy, or Simon the groundskeeper, bent double, sweeping the sidewalks all around the house with a bundle of stiff straw.

First the sound is a dry swishing, sweeping off yesterday's rust-colored dust, wilted flowers, and pieces of gravel. Then the swishing is wet, as he makes his dutiful round again, this time with a basin of water, dipping his broom in and washing the long sidewalk and our front steps, leaving them wet and clean when we get up and unlock the doors to let in the morning light and air and begin our day.

We are still raw newcomers in Africa, slack-jawed at the sights, feeling our way around, overwhelmed with the differences.

Yet, in little ways it is becoming like home. Every day, I see small things that remind me of Oregon, and the strange and new are gradually becoming familiar.

My husband Paul and our five children and I began this four-month project—helping a small organization called Into Africa with its work with orphaned boys. Rick McAninch, the director of Into Africa, drove us the 200 miles from the airport in the capital, Nairobi, to Kisumu.

Along the way, gasps from the children alerted me to two baboons squatting beside the road, and farther on, a herd of zebras grazed nearby. We drove through the famous Rift Valley, where it seems a giant knife sliced down the western third of Kenya and pried the two sides far apart.

As we drove through villages, women sat patiently beside the road, hoping to sell us carrots stuffed into plastic bags or potatoes stacked in neat pyramids.

Trees grew on many of the hillsides, their shapes familiar from a lifetime of *National Geographic* photographs of African sunsets with silhouetted giraffes among flaring, flat-topped trees.

About halfway to Kisumu and still in the hills, we started seeing what looked like vast fields full of bushy plants in a vivid spring green. It's tea, Rick told us, first cultivated here by the British and now a major export.

In Oregon, a field that size would probably be harvested by a big John Deere combine, but here, the tea fields are all harvested by hand, the workers picking off the newest leaves and putting them in baskets on their backs.

After a jarring five-hour ride on some of the worst roads I have ever seen, we reached Kisumu and our new home.

With nearly a million people, Kisumu is the third-largest city in Kenya. Located just south of the equator, it hugs the north shore of a small arm off Lake Victoria, the second-largest freshwater lake in the world and the source of the Nile River.

Having viewed it from across the bay, I would guess that the area of the city is far less than Eugene, with its 140,000-some population.

The only way to describe Kisumu is as I first saw it—a series of vivid impressions coming too rapidly to process them fully. Swarms of people—walking beside the road, milling down the sidewalks—the crowd at the Harrisburg parade repeated every day.

Very few cars in relation to the number of people on foot. Tiny little stores packed next to each other, selling electronics or dishes or bread.

Crowded white minibuses called *matatus*, careening down the street, their musical horns honking wildly. Small rickety fruit stands on street corners, the roofs consisting of skinny parallel branches.

Feverish beggars pleading, "My mother in Mombasa is very sick. Please, I need money for food for her." Street boys slinking up to your car, hands extended.

Women in bright dresses carrying umbrellas to shade them from the sun. Bicycle taxis whizzing by with each passenger straddling a seat behind the driver much like you probably used to ride with your big brother.

For most people in Kisumu, life is very difficult. Blue-collar wages run between one and three U.S. dollars a day. Malaria is so common that the U.S. Center for Disease Control does much of its malaria research here. The AIDS statistics are vague but terrible by all accounts, with an estimated 20 to 25 percent of the population inflicted with HIV or AIDS.

Corruption robs people of a fair chance to get ahead, and bribery is so rampant that public places such as airports are festooned with signs: "You have the right to be served. DO NOT OFFER A BRIBE."

Upstairs the Peasants are Revolting

Our three-bedroom apartment is an escape from the overwhelming realities of the street. It is part of a sprawling concrete house that contains the office and library of Into Africa, the directors and their family, and half a dozen staff members.

Surrounded by high walls and hedges for security reasons, our home is located in a lovely middle-class section of town with American-sized houses, well-kept flower beds, palm and mango trees, and neat driveways where gardeners slowly sweep the flower petals off the gravel in the hot afternoon sun.

This part of Kisumu is where little familiar touches of home pop up unexpectedly—a philodendron just like my potted plant at home, a prowling cat. Paul and I went on a walk one day and came up behind a herd of cows ambling along the street exactly like the cows in Minnesota used to meander home when I rounded them up at milking time.

Just a few blocks away, in stark contrast to our manicured section of town, is one of Kisumu's three slums, a vast field of tightly-packed makeshift shacks, dirt paths, old galvanized tin roofing, painted advertisements, and people, people, people.

A hundred thousand people live there, they say, but I wonder who could ever get an accurate count. Here, more than anywhere else in the city, the poverty reaches out and slaps us in our sheltered American faces.

Every morning, thousands of people walk from this slum, past our gate, to their jobs downtown, a mile away. To our amazement, they are, almost without exception, neat and clean—the men in slacks and buttoned shirts; the women in pretty dresses or well-pressed skirts and blouses.

And when I meet them, the people are friendly, smiling, and nodding. From my perspective, it seems impossible.

Still a newcomer, I wonder if I will ever really understand these mysterious images of Kenya: clean and friendly people somehow emerging from a horrifying slum. A thousand strange new sights mixed with a dozen dear and familiar.

And waking every morning to sweeping brooms—the sound of a strong and quiet dignity refusing to give in to dirt and despair and desperation, the sound of daily swishing bravely on.

Making a difference

It was said, in the concentration camps of Europe in World War II, that among great cruelty and inhumanity one could also find great kindness and sacrifice.

Here in Africa, where daily life for many people is somewhere between difficult and horrifying, one finds small flames glowing—people willing to sacrifice to make a difference. Compelled by what they sense as a "call" from God, they do what they can, undaunted by the enormous suffering around them, content to make a difference to a few. We have been honored to get to know some of these special people and watch them at work.

According to our new friend Vincent Okello, a walking almanac of Kenyan statistics, all the indicators of poverty in Kenya are up in the past five years.

"More people than ever are living on less than one U.S. dollar a day," he says. "And it is always the children who are affected first. More of them die before the age of five, fewer get an education, and girls marry younger and carry on the cycle of poverty."

We asked Vincent about the street boys we see downtown. "How do they get there? Are they dumped like abandoned puppies at the age of eight or 10?"

"No," he says. "There is a three- to five-year pattern of increasing neglect before they end up on the street. Often the father is sick first, and the mother is increasingly preoccupied with his care, perhaps leaving to visit him in the hospital. Then after he dies, she is preoccupied with earning a living and getting food, and the child is left alone more and more, and perhaps the mother also dies. The child begins to make forays to the neighbors to ask for food, then he goes farther afield, then to the nearest town, then to the next one, and finally he ends up here on the streets of Kisumu."

Vincent is a college graduate—a rarity here, as fewer than one percent of Kenyans earns a degree. "I could easily leave and get a job in Europe or America," he says. "All of my friends have left. But I feel called of God to stay here and help my country."

He has a good job doing research for a non-government organization working with technology development. In addition, he donates his time to a number of causes, serving on committees with the Kenya Bureau of Standards and Save the Children UK. He also is the administrator of Into Africa, helping Rick and Audrey McAninch and the 30-plus street boys in their care.

Rick McAninch was a successful sales manager for a wholesale plumbing company in Seattle before he and Audrey came to Kenya in 1995. Now, he takes care of a hundred nuts-and-bolts details for Into Africa, and she oversees the boys' daily care and education.

At the Timothy House, the boys' home and school, the boys cook on a fire outside and sleep on no-frills metal bunk beds.

"We don't want them to get accustomed to an American lifestyle," Audrey says, "because they will probably never be able to maintain it in this country after they're grown, and there's almost no chance they can go to Europe or America. So we want them to know how to survive in this culture. But mostly we try to build the character and practical skills that can make them leaders, so they can be like David in the Bible, who started off as a shepherd but had what it took to be a king when the time was right."

Kenya's educational system and widespread corruption make finding capable teachers and trustworthy staff difficult. The rewards, says Audrey, are seeing a boy who people think would never be anybody and watching him become somebody, and seeing the change in boys' eyes, from the vacant look one sees on the street to "happy eyes."

When we first arrived in Kisumu, and were still sorting out all the new faces, Audrey said, "Jonas is gone right now, but you'll know he's back when you hear singing."

Sure enough, a few days later, I heard a gospel song in a rich baritone, vibrating around a corner. Behind it came a tall young man, all knees and elbows, with a big smile. It was 25-year-old Jonas, who grew up in a nearby village and has been helping the McAninches for nearly eight years.

Jonas helps to screen the boys who come to Into Africa. He gets to know them on the street and travels to their home villages to determine if they are really orphans and if family members could care for them. While he would love to make a living performing gospel music, Jonas's calling for now is with the street boys, teaching music and serving as a houseparent at the Timothy House.

He also goes downtown early in the morning, when the boys are waking up from their night on the sidewalks, to let them know help is available. At times he rounds up several dozen, takes them to a restaurant, and buys them bean-and-corn porridge.

Once a week, Jonas goes to the Remand Center, a government-sponsored rescue/juvenile detention center. My husband accompanied him one Friday and watched, amazed, as Jonas sang and talked for two hours and kept the full attention of 60 kids.

One day, we heard a commotion at the gate and found that it was Jonas and five new boys just off the street. Soon Audrey, a drill sergeant of a woman with a big heart, was behind the house "interviewing" them.

"Can you work? We don't want boys here that don't work!"

Yeah, they could all work, they said. She handed each a garbage bag and told them to prove it, so they trooped out the gate and down the street to fill their bags with garbage. After a while, they returned, looking like tired, raggedy Santas with packs on their backs.

We went outside to meet the boys, and it was like an Aid-for-Africa brochure come to life. Imagine a boy, per-haps your 10-year-old son, in an ancient pair of shorts and an old T-shirt, five sizes too big, gray with dirt, shoulders ripping out. Imagine the look in the eyes of a boy with no mom, no dad, no home, no love, no bed to sleep in, no food in the fridge; a boy who regularly sniffs solvents to forget his troubles; who has spent the last year fending for him-self on the streets at the mercy of the weather and older boys preying on him in the sickest ways imaginable.

It was those eyes that stuck a knife in my gut and twisted it.

Thankfully, Audrey decided they could all stay, and Jonas escorted them to their new home and got them settled in. Within a few weeks, the boys' vacant eyes began to change into the eyes of normal, mischievous 10-year-olds.

Jonas also helped our family get acquainted with Kisumu. A few days after we arrived, he offered to show us the neighborhood. We wandered around the block and down another street and ended up at New Life Home.

Some years ago, a British couple saw the need for a place in Nairobi for abandoned babies and those with HIV/AIDS, so they opened the first New Life Home. Later, they wanted to start satellite homes in other cities, so Rick and Audrey offered part of their house. Two years ago, the babies were moved to a new building about a half-mile away.

We entered the gate and signed in with the guard. Then, a nurse named Prisca showed us around.

"We have 16 babies now," she said. "We find them every-where—in garbage cans, in latrines, left beside the road, abandoned at hospitals and police stations. We keep them here until they're six months old. Most of them get adopted out—over half to Kenyans and the rest to Europe and America."

We entered a breezy room and saw a receptionist's desk, couches for visitors, and half a dozen babies in infant seats. The place was clean and neat and sunny and well-furnished—but I took one look at those beautiful babies and felt an enormous and terrible sorrow rising up inside of me, and I burst into tears.

Prisca was still talking, but I was drowning in tears and trying to find a tissue.

"I'm sorry," I told her. "I can't help it."

"I understand," Prisca said kindly. "It's very moving. I've lived in Kenya all my life, and I still see things that move me to tears."

Four years ago, Prisca had a good job at the best hospital in town. But, she says, "I was reaching the end of the road with stress. All the deaths, all the HIV...I saw that I couldn't take it anymore. Then our friends Rick and Audrey asked if

I would help with the babies, and I felt called to this work. The pay is less, but it's much more satisfying. The babies come in so sick, and after a few days they perk up. You see them grow, then you see them get adopted into a family, and the parents bring them back to visit. It's so rewarding."

Prisca's husband John was a banker with Kenya Commercial Bank, but after Prisca began her work with the babies, he says, he felt called to help as well. He is now the administrator, overseeing the finances and general operation of New Life Home, Kisumu. "When you do what God wants you to do," John and Prisca say, "you are always at peace."

Kenya has nearly a million AIDS orphans, Kisumu has 1,500 street boys, and the AIDS infection rate is still increasing. Somehow undaunted by the statistics around them, these ordinary people are quietly making a difference in people's lives, one by one.

Another tiny grave

One Sunday, we got a taste of life—and death—in an African village.

There are Mennonite churches in five villages surrounding Kisumu, so we decided to attend the one in Rabuor, about 15 minutes away, on the main road leading to Nairobi. When we called the pastor's wife to get directions, she said that they were having only a short service at church that morning. After that, they would all be going to a funeral at the home of one of their church members, a young family whose five-month-old son had died the previous Friday.

After a brief service in a simple, concrete-block building, everyone piled into all the available vehicles as only Africans can pile into vehicles. Our family sat in our dusty Peugeot station wagon's two seats, and three grown men squeezed into the back. We made a small caravan as we headed down the main road.

After a few minutes, we turned off onto a dirt road and bumped along for a few more dusty miles, then parked beside a swamp.

Our group of 30 or 40 gathered at the bridge that crossed the swamp. It was probably 50 feet long, and we inched across, picking our way cautiously along the haphazard collection of branches and boards, careful not to step on the end of a board for fear it would plunge down, seesaw style. Thankfully, there were fenceposts every 10 feet or so to grab onto, and to my relief the pastor picked up Jenny, my four-year-old daughter, and carried her across.

After we had all safely crossed the swamp, we walked across a large cow pasture—dotted with thorn bushes and, here and there, a spindly tree—over to a circle of houses in a *dala*, or family group. Traditionally, the husband has a house, and each wife has a house, and later, the sons add houses as they are married. There is a complicated hierarchy, and a specific way each house has to face in relation to the others.

The parents of the deceased child were Tom and Goretty. They had a total of seven children, and this one, little Merle Beachy, named after a Mennonite bishop, was the fourth to die. He was sick for four days, they said. They assumed it was malaria.

First, we went to Tom and Goretty's place, crowding into the dark interior of their 20-square-foot house with its thick mud walls and corrugated metal roof. We stood around the little coffin and sang a few hymns in the Luo language.

Next, we were told to go outside to a makeshift shelter about 50 feet away, where old metal chairs and couches with foam rubber cushions were arranged in a semicircle. Three or four posts had been stuck in the ground, and a few ropes were strung between them and a thorn tree. Then, reed mats and burlap were laid on the ropes to make a bit of shade.

Our family was ushered to the best seats, the little coffin was placed on a small table directly in front of me, and the mother was seated in a chair nearby.

Other people filtered in—more church people, neighbors, family. They found places under the shelter or under the thorn trees nearby. There was no wailing, no noise, almost no talking.

The service began, again with Luo hymns. As the funeral proceeded through a sermon and testimonies and more songs, I sat there with the sun burning hotter and hotter through the thin burlap above me, and felt like I was tasting a little bit of this family's suffering.

There was Goretty in her blue dress, sitting calmly nearby. And there in the center of the canopy lay the body of her precious little boy in a cheap wooden coffin with a window in the top that allowed us to see him without smelling the odors of a two-day-old unembalmed body in the dreadful heat. Across from us sat Tom, on a couch with a few other men, his face deeply sad but also calm. Their three-year-old son laid his head on his mother's chair and fell asleep.

Far away, near another *dala*, a small boy chased his cows among the thorn bushes. The sun burned relentlessly. A rooster crowed. Once in a while, a slight breeze whiffed through the shelter; otherwise, the heat surrounded us like a smothering cloud. A sick-looking brown dog, with open sores on his back and all his ribs showing, crept under the pastor's chair and fell asleep.

I thought back to the night before, when our family had driven out to Lake Victoria. On the way home, we were talking about mosquitoes, and Jenny, with her usual vivid imagination, was devising ways to get rid of them.

"I'm going to draw a picture of a lizard, 'cuz lizards eat mosquitoes, and then I'll show it to the mosquitoes and say 'Rarrr!' to scare them away."

"But lizards don't say 'Rarrr!'" her sister said.

"I know. But I'll just say it to scare the mosquitoes," Jenny said.

It was completely unfair, I decided, that by virtue of where I was born, I could enjoy my daughter and watch her grow up. And, if the mosquitoes didn't all get chased off and she did get malaria, we had the city's best labs and doctors and pharmacies at our disposal. Goretty, by being born in an out-of-the-way African village, could never get her hopes up that her babies would live long enough to talk or draw pictures or grow into adulthood. Indeed, something as diagnosable and curable as malaria had just killed her baby.

This, I thought, is a tragedy.

The service was very quiet. The funeral processions that often pass our house in Kisumu are noisy with screaming, wailing, and what sounds like people banging pots and pans. There were tears at this funeral, but no screaming. To my amazement, both Tom and Goretty stood up and spoke for a few minutes. I couldn't understand what they were saying, but their voices were calm and they seemed to be filled with a supernatural grace.

The service drew to a close, and it was time for the burial. There are no cemeteries as such in the villages; family members are buried in the *dala*. We filed solemnly by Tom and Goretty's house, and there, 10 feet behind their house, was a four-foot-deep hole in the black dirt, with the coffin already in it by the time we got there. The bishop for whom the baby had been named said a few words of comfort to the family and encouraged the church to support them.

"Ashes to ashes," he said. "Earth to earth." And he dropped the first handful of dirt in the grave. It landed with a hollow thump.

I thought, Four times. Four times, now, this mother has buried a child. I am 41 years old, and I can't even remember ever attending the funeral of a child. And this young woman has now personally buried four.

The group dispersed after the burial, waiting, subdued, for lunch. The food was served on plastic plates and eaten with plastic spoons—a scoop of white rice with another scoop of boiled pinto beans. We sat in the scant shade of the houses and ate, then left for home, a long line of us filing across the cow pasture in the blazing sunshine.

We crossed the dubious bridge and piled into our vehicles, this time squeezing five grown men in the back of the Peugeot. We dropped the men off along the way and before long, we were home again, where our apartment had never seemed so cool and welcoming, and we had cold drinks and showers and naps. By evening, most of us were glowing with radiant pink sunburns.

Looking back, I think what I will remember even more than the terrible heat and sadness of that place are the faces of Tom and Goretty. In spite of their losses, they still held firmly to their faith, with a look of calm, quiet trust that God is with them and knows what he's doing.

When life and hope flourish in Kenya, I believe it will be God and people like Tom and Goretty who bring it about.

Bubbles and paper airplanes

There is a saying, "Be careful what you wish for; you might get it."

Before I was married, I taught in a church school. One of my worst "hardships" was those pesky parents. One mother thought I was too hard on her child, another thought I wasn't teaching good penmanship, and another didn't like the stories I read to the children. I would share these woes with my friends and conclude, "I wish I could just teach a bunch of orphans! Then I wouldn't have to deal with parents."

Twenty years later, my wish came true, and of course it wasn't at all what I thought it would be. Teaching African orphans turned my assumptions upside down. At the same time, the boys blessed me in ways that jaded American kids could never do.

The 30 former street boys at Into Africa's Timothy House in Kisumu range in age from approximately 10 to 17. They attend school right on the premises, and those who are unable to read are put through a phonics course before joining the main classroom.

During our months in Kenya, my husband Paul taught the larger group of boys and trained two teachers to take over when he left. I helped two or three hours a week with the six boys in the learning-to-read class. First, the teacher wanted me to help him teach phonics, but I soon found out that with the Kenyan rolled or silent R's and all-purpose "ah" sound for vowels, it made no sense for an American to teach them sounds. Instead, I introduced them to a variety of crafts and activities, a good way for them to learn English, motor skills, and much more.

We painted a color wheel on the first day and I found that as long as the boys understood my English, they followed directions very well. "Blue in this section, yellow in that one, and then we mix blue and yellow ...."

"Iss gdeen!" hollered Steven, the youngest, his face lighting up with joy.

This, I found, was the most rewarding part of teaching—their sense of discovery, their exuberant wonder. I had assumed that every 12-year-old boy on the planet had at some point made a paper airplane and tossed it across a classroom. But these boys had never heard of paper airplanes, and they frowned intensely as they tried to follow my example, folding this corner down to that line and pressing it down. Then they stood in a line and tossed their planes, a look of priceless amazement on their faces as the planes swooped away.

We made three sizes of airplanes—tiny, medium, and huge—and I told them to guess which would fly farthest. This was their most difficult challenge—thinking for themselves. Their scant education in the Kenyan system had all been rote memorization, and it seemed that no one had ever asked them questions to really make them think.

But they remembered well and even taught the older boys, because Paul told me later that after that lesson, he sometimes confiscated an errant paper airplane in the main classroom.

We mixed dish soap, water, and glycerin one day, I gave each boy a piece of wire to bend into a bubble wand, and then we went outside for their first experience with blowing bubbles. Little Jentrice swished his wand through the air and hollered "Thdee!" as three bubbles wafted through the air. Some of the older boys, 16- and 17-year-olds, watched curiously. I gave them pieces of wire and soon they also discovered, for the first time, the thrill of sending a glistening soap bubble through the air.

I also had assumed that all children know how to use scissors. But the first time we had a paper-cutting project, I was shocked to see two of the boys awkwardly chomping the blades at the paper, their fingers stiff and straight. So I found myself showing a 14-year-old how to use scissors, curving his fingers this way and his thumb like that, all the while thinking, This can't be.

Lurking behind the joys of teaching was the dark awareness that these boys were orphans with terribly painful pasts. One day, I decided to teach them "people" words with stick figures on the blackboard. Man, woman, boy, girl. "The man is the boy's father," I said. "The girl is his sister."

And then I turned around and for the first time saw hard and haunted looks on the boys' faces. What was I thinking, to wander into this minefield, talking of dads and sisters to boys who had lost their families?

"I don't know your stories," I finally said, "but I know you have had hard times and your lives have been sad. But in the Bible, God says that he loves you and he will be a father to you. So when you are sad, you can tell him all about it, and he will hear you." And then I wrapped up the class and fled, burdened with their collective grief.

When I had taught in other schools, we made trivets for the kids' mothers, and most of their artwork went home to hang on the refrigerator or be mailed to Grandma. What do you do with an orphan's artwork?

Well, they had other caring adults in their lives such as houseparents and teachers, so one day we rubber-stamped thank-you notes. Following my example, Lawrence tapped a stamp on the ink pad, carefully pressed it on his paper, and lifted it off. "Caht!" he shouted, thrilled with the image on his paper.

"When people do things for us, we thank them," I said. "It makes them happy. So on these cards, we will write a message saying thank you to the people who take care of you." Jentrice waved his hand in the air and desperately tried to express himself in English. "I thank *you*, Teachah, for coming to teach us!" he exclaimed.

That was supposed to make me happy, but instead, whenever I think of his words, I cry. I am now back in my normal American routine, but my heart is still back with "my" street boys. In my vast abundance, I remember how little they had, how much they gave, and how blessed I was to know them.

Bread on the waters

I first noticed Steven the day he limped into class. He was about nine years old, the youngest in the learning-to-read group at the boys' home in Kisumu. Steven was limping, it turned out, because he had an oozing, open wound near his ankle.

This child, I thought, examining his foot, needs a mother.

He continued to catch my eye with his quiet smile and little bursts of enthusiasm, such as his delighted "Iss gdeen!" when he mixed blue and yellow paint.

Before we went to Kenya, we had talked about adopting a baby. Helping for an hour once a week at the babies' orphanage, I wanted every baby in the place. Yet we never felt that deep-inside "yes" necessary for such a decision.

Then one day while my husband and I were driving to school, I said impulsively, "Maybe we should adopt Steven."

Where did that come from? I wondered afterward. I really hadn't planned to say it.

To my surprise, Paul thought it was a wonderful idea, and our five children were just as enthusiastic. They soon thought of all kinds of reasons we should adopt.

Some were silly: It's so much easier to cut a pie into eight pieces rather than seven, and just think, a package of eight hot dogs would come out even.

Other reasons were practical: Our house is big enough for another child. He would fit neatly into the five-year empty slot between Ben and Jenny. He needs a family, and we have the resources to provide one for him.

Fundamentally, we all sensed that we could not experience Kenya's orphan crisis firsthand and not do something tangible about it, something beyond giving our time for a few months.

Ideally, we would have found a Kenyan family to take Steven, and helped with his ongoing expenses. But the AIDS situation is so advanced that the system is saturated, and anyone with any means is already taking care of nieces, nephews, and other relatives.

Even though adoption had been my idea, I had the most misgivings. Was it wise to make a poor black Kenyan Pentecostal city child part of a comfortable white American rural Mennonite family? Steven was a happy child; was it right to uproot him? Did I have enough energy to meet the needs of six children, and was Paul too busy to be a dad to another child?

"What if we adopt him and I don't like him?" I asked Paul one morning.

He snorted. "Do you always like me?"

"No," I admitted. End of discussion.

"Think of the future," suggested our Kenyan friend Vincent. "You know the Smucker family will still be a family in five years. No one knows if this boys' home will still be here then."

One morning, Paul read from Ecclesiastes 11:1, 2 for our family's Bible time: "Cast thy bread upon the waters: for thou shalt find it after many days. Give a portion to seven, and also to eight; for thou knowest not what evil shall be upon the earth."

Fifteen-year-old Amy's face lit up. "That's it! There's our sign!" I assumed she meant the part about casting bread on the waters, but I was wrong. "See?" she said. "It says, 'Give a portion to seven' and we're seven now, 'and also to eight,' and if we get Steven, we'll be eight!"

At first we laughed—such twisting of scripture. But the more I thought about it, the more I felt like that verse was meant for us that morning. Casting your bread on the waters meant investing your resources even when the outcome is uncertain. We didn't know "what evil shall be upon the earth" and how, at some point, we could bless Steven's life, and he ours. We returned to the United States in March, determined to pray and ask for advice before we made a decision.

One week in April, we specifically asked God for "no's" and closed doors if we shouldn't do this. All we got were resounding "yes's" and doors flying open.

Steven's AIDS test came back negative, and an investigator was unable to locate any relatives at all (we didn't want to adopt unless he was a "total" orphan). I had an unexpected conversation with two adoptive moms at a garage sale, where I mentioned what we were thinking and my uncertainty about it.

"Do you remember his eyes?" one of the women asked me, a wise and knowing look on her face. And I immediately started crying; I remembered his eyes all too well.

We e-mailed Paul's African-American cousin for advice and he responded enthusiastically, offering to help in any way he could. "If any family can do this successfully, the Smuckers can," he wrote.

Other people cautioned us with chilling unsuccessful-adoption stories and wondered how we would deal with racial issues. How can we do this? I would ask myself, panicking. And then I would wonder, more calmly, How can we *not* do this?

Eventually, we knew this was the right thing to do, a deep-inside "yes" that would give us strength for the long process ahead.

We waited to tell him until the home study and other paperwork were completed, then the home's director informed Steven and e-mailed his response. "I'm happy. I feel good—to live with you. I want to be their son. I want to be with brothers and sisters. I feel good to have them."

And then, finally, it was real—Steven was going to be our son. My birth-children began with a seed in my womb; Steven became my son through a seed planted in my heart the day I looked at his foot and realized how much he needed a mother.

I once heard a woman say that joy and sorrow travel on the same track and arrive at the same time. We completed the paperwork to adopt Steven and bought a ticket for Paul to fly to Kenya. At the same time, Paul's dad fought his battle with cancer, enduring four weeks of daily radiation. As Paul's departure date drew closer, his dad grew weaker, and our lives were a strange mixture of anticipation and dread.

Should Paul go or shouldn't he? we wondered. The all-important court date was set and we both felt we shouldn't cancel it unless we absolutely had to.

On the day we were preparing to leave for the airport, I was dashing around looking for books Paul could read on the plane. Then the phone rang. It was Paul's youngest sister. "Dad's gone," she said simply.

Instead of flying off to meet his new son, Paul was canceling his flights and appointments and making funeral arrangements for his father.

We grieved for Paul's dad, for our plans, and for Steven's hopes—he had been so excited about seeing his new dad. It would be several months, we figured, before a new court date could be arranged.

To our surprise, our lawyer in Kenya arranged for a new court date only two weeks later. From that point on, we had an increasing sense that God was in charge of this script, writing the story, and that we were only characters in it, woven in with circumstances and miracles far beyond our control.

On the Internet, we had found a group of parents who adopted in Kenya. "It can take months," they warned us. "You'll never get those documents without bribing. I had to give this guy $200 in a men's restroom with the lights off." "The people at the embassy are heartless—you'll be their lowest priority and they really don't care what happens to you." "An embassy inspector has to travel from Nairobi to Kisumu to do an investigation. That can delay things for weeks."

Nevertheless, Paul bought tickets for both him and Steven to return to America on Christmas Eve, three weeks after he left.

Here in Oregon, the church youth group gathered at 11 p.m. to pray at the same time the court hearing was taking place in Kenya. The judge approved the adoption, and Steven was officially ours.

Our lawyer, we found out later, was astonished. The day before, he had appeared before the judge and presented what he thought was an open-and-shut adoption case—a Kenyan couple wanted to adopt the wife's niece. But the judge refused to approve the adoption. There was no chance, the lawyer thought, that the judge would let this American man adopt a 10-year-old Kenyan boy.

A woman at the American embassy took a personal interest in Steven's case and did all she could to get his visa. She also did the investigation.

"My family is from that area," she said. "I have to attend a funeral near Kisumu on Saturday, so I'll come by and do the investigation on Sunday."

Doors opened at the right time, planes flew to Nairobi on schedule, and a vast network of friends kept praying that Paul and Steven could be home for Christmas.

Five years ago, after our daughter Jenny was born, I told Paul, "You can have the next baby!"

In a very real sense, that was exactly what happened. While I stayed at home and encouraged from a distance, Paul labored through regulations, forms, waiting in lines, and computer glitches that threatened delays—all without bribing anyone.

He also bonded with his new son, telling me excitedly about the first time that Steven called him "Dad" and Steven's reaction to seeing giraffes for the first time, out the window of the train.

At the Portland airport, on Christmas Eve, we met Paul and Steven in a flood of hugs and tears.

Since then, Steven has been learning what it means to be part of a family. He feeds the cat every morning, colors pictures with five-year-old Jenny, and hugs me goodnight.

Every day, he makes new discoveries—riding a bike, seeing fog and frost for the first time, sticking magnets to the refrigerator, and picking out "Joy to the World" on the piano.

"He sounds exactly like a Smucker," says my friend Arlene.

Of course he does—that's exactly who he is.

Normal, with a twist

Every six weeks, the guys in our family get haircuts. I roll up the bathroom rug, set up a wooden stool, clip a garbage bag around their shoulders, and snip. First, Paul's thinning blond hair falls to the floor. Matt's thick auburn hair is next on the pile, then Ben's dark brown locks.

Steven was 10 years old and bald when we adopted him in December—they shaved the boys' heads at the orphanage as a precaution against lice. We let his hair grow, letting it form a soft black fluff and learning how to care for it from helpful people at Sally Beauty Supply.

Finally, Steven's hair began to gather in untidy clumps, and it was time for his first haircut. We followed the same 20-year-ritual of setting him on the stool and clipping the garbage bag with a clothespin. But what should I do then? With the others, I always flip tufts of hair up between my fingers with a comb and then cut them off. But each strand of Steven's hair was like a tightly-coiled spring. There was no way I could use the same technique.

Finally, I pushed the comb into a clump of hair, flat against his head, and cut off everything above the comb, repeating the process all over his scalp. Instead of feathery strands drifting to the floor, little black wads of fluff dropped down, and I pronounced his slightly-uneven trim a success.

Since we save samples of each first haircut for the baby books, we gathered Steven's hair into a little Ziploc bag, labeled it, and put it away.

This, I decided, is life with Steven: normal—but with just a slight twist.

For the first few weeks, Steven was alarmingly good. Quiet and cooperative, he ate what was set in front of him and went to bed when he was told. Not that I minded having an easy child, but I worried that he was too damaged by his past to be a "real" child.

Then, the night our church hosted a welcoming party for him, I found out he was a normal boy. Two or three little girls came running down the stairs, shrieking that Steven was balancing on the balcony rail. I nearly fainted, imagining him plunging 15 feet down and cracking his head open on the edge of an oak pew. Even though he had spent the past four years in an all-male environment, Steven obviously had an inborn urge to show off for girls.

He also, it turned out, had the same compulsion that my other two boys were born with to throw balls in the living room. And, like his brothers at age 10, he thought all noisy bodily functions were hilariously funny.

Just as I was convinced that he was a normal 10-year-old Smucker boy, he threw in a little twist, choosing a purple comb-and-mirror set from the merit store in his classroom and proudly wearing the comb in his hair. It was hard to know how to respond—should I let him enjoy the comb and expose him to possible ridicule, or should I disappoint him with an explanation of American gender roles?

It also was hard, at first, to set limits or to discipline Steven. Thinking of his past, with its unimaginable grief and loss, was almost paralyzing. Somehow, I wanted to spare him pain for the rest of his life. So, with sweetness and patience, I explained the family rules: "In this house, we walk around the couch, like this; we do not climb over it, and we do not throw balls in the living room because things can break."

Then, quite suddenly, I was tired of being syrupy. Steven was a member of the family; he ought to get the same treatment as anyone else. So when he threw his red ball in the living room again and it hit the ceiling fan and light with a clanging of chains and fan blades, he got yelled at with all three names: "Steven Ochieng Smucker!"

After that, he was like a lamb let loose in a new pasture—having a wonderful time but determined to test the electric fences and getting shocked every time. He went down to the creek without telling me where he was going. No creek time for two days. He got his church pants muddy. ("I didn't play outside. Really. I only ran around.") No electronic time for two days.

Then, when I thought he was getting causes and effects all figured out, he showed me how little he really knew. He had the good sense to take off his new watch before washing the car, but then he tossed it in the grass and forgot to pick it up. It was run over by the lawn mower and destroyed. I grieved more than he did when he gathered up the broken pieces and brought them inside. How I wanted to rush out and replace the watch, but we knew he would learn faster if we let him experience the consequences.

In matters such as the watch, Steven reasoned like a four-year-old. My other five children progressed through childhood in logical stages—fun babies, exploring toddlers, inquisitive preschoolers, and so on.

Steven still seems to experience every stage of childhood at once. He snuggles beside me to listen to *The Biggest Bear* over and over, just like my kids at age three. He giggled like a six-month-old and begged for more when I showed him how This Little Piggy was done. For weeks, he was like a two-year-old, dashing around the house, grabbing everything he could reach, and pushing buttons on the phone, computer, and CD player while I followed with a chorus of no-no's. He dug a hole in the garden and had a mud fight with Ben like any 10-year-old.

And sometimes, sadly, Steven is about 30 years old.

One day, my daughters were discussing a character in an Anne of Green Gables book. "In the book, the boy dies. In the movie, he lives," one of them said.

Steven, overhearing, got a frightened look in his eyes.

"Who died?" he asked.

"Just a pretend person in a book," I said. Then, on a hunch, I added, "Did any of your friends die when you lived on the street?"

"There was a big boy who wanted to be the leader of the street boys," he answered. "And some of the others didn't like him. So they took a block like this," (demonstrating about two feet by three feet) "and they threw it at him. A lady took him to the hospital and they buried him."

It was the familiar twist, only this time it was a knife twisting in my gut. God have mercy, I thought, how can we ever hope to heal this child's soul? Within minutes, however, Steven was back to normal—shooting baskets, playing with the cat, doing his chores—his happy look back in his eyes.

Our prayer for Steven is that somewhere among the siblings and parents and pets and food and love and friends that make up his world now, the gaps in his life will be filled in and he will emerge as a normal, functional adult. Yet, we also want him to stay just a bit on the other side of normal, with his grief and loss turned into an extra measure of compassion, his pain becoming a greater sense of gratitude and joy.

A boy and his dog

Our adopted son Steven is just like the rest of the Smuckers in that he has a noisy sneeze and can argue like a budding lawyer, but he also has a heart for animals like none of us has ever seen.

The girls and I like cats, and in his early teens our oldest son Matt was fond of his lizards in a detached, scientific way. But for the most part we are not animal lovers, and in particular, I am not a dog person.

But Steven loves all animals and has a gentle, mysterious charm with them. Last winter, he found a half-dead rabbit on the road, brought it inside, and tried to revive it. Even though my husband Paul insists that Katzie is an outdoor cat, Steven sneaks out the back door on cold mornings and lets her into the laundry room.

We had the house re-sided last summer, and one day the siding guy, whom I had considered a sensible man up to that point, found two half-grown starlings in the porch rafters. He gave them to Steven, suggesting he keep them as pets. I was unaware of this until I came into the living room and saw two birds fluttering madly in opposite directions and a flustered and guilty-looking Steven trying to chase down both at once.

We finally corralled the birds and put them outside, Steven helped me clean up their deposits on the carpet, and I lectured him about keeping wild animals out of doors. He complied, reluctantly, and after that I would see him sitting motionless on the porch swing with the starlings on his shoulders.

But he always wanted more animals. He begged for chickens, lambs, more cats. Cows and horses would be nice, and goats. Maybe some ducks and turkeys. And a dog. He really, really wanted a dog.

The biggest drawback to having animals is the guilt I endure when the kids lose interest and neglect them. Matt still cringes when I bring up the Dead Hamster Episode that led to the end of his pet career.

The last thing I wanted was the guilt of a dirty, hungry dog yapping at the back door. "I have enough to take care of around here without adding a dog to the list," I ranted, but my protests did not decrease the pleading look in Steven's eyes, or his siblings', who were rapidly being swayed to his side.

"All right," Paul told Steven, "you prove with Katzie that you can take care of a pet, and we'll get you a dog." There wasn't much to prove, I admitted, grudgingly, as Steven had been feeding Katzie faithfully almost from the day he arrived.

Paul thought we should get a dog from a shelter or the "free" ads in the newspaper, maybe after Christmas. But then we heard about Mr. Fenske's dog.

Mr. Fenske was an elderly German man from nearby Brownsville who started attending our church. One Sunday I asked him, "*Wie geht's?*" ("How's it going?") He grinned in delight, and we had a short conversation. I looked forward to practicing my German with him again, but he died only a short time later.

The family asked the church youth group to sing at his funeral. Not long after, we were told that Mr. Fenske had left a dog, and his children wanted to give it to one of those Mennonite families whose young people sang so nicely at the funeral.

Oh, great.

We drove to Brownsville one Saturday to see the dog. Mr. Fenske's son Daniel led us through the house and onto the back porch where we were greeted by a massive beast that looked the size and color of the lions we saw on safari in Kenya.

"No. Absolutely not," I protested mentally. "He could pick up Jenny and toss her like a rag doll. If he planted those paws on my chest I'd be flat on my back in an instant."

"His name is Hansie, and he's real friendly," Daniel said. Indeed. Hansie pranced around us, sniffing impolitely and wagging his tail so hard it nearly knocked us over. To my relief, he didn't lick, bite, or jump up on us, but we soon had dirt and blond hairs all over our clothes from waist to shoes.

"My dad was too weak to groom him much," the son apologized. I could well imagine. Two grown men couldn't bathe this dog against his will, and for sure not frail Mr. Fenske with his walker.

"I suppose he'd eat us out of house and home," I muttered.

"Actually, he doesn't eat that much," Daniel said. "The last time we weighed him he was 180 pounds, so we're cutting down on his food."

We drove home with the kids bouncing up and down in the back seat. "Yes! Yes! Yes! Let's get him!" Paul kept his own counsel, but I could tell he loved the dog and was plotting his strategy for persuading me.

The next few days, Paul organized and the children promised: food, shelter, water, grooming, playtime, cleanup, training. Delicately they chipped away at my resistance until I had to admit that I had no more reason to say no.

Except for one thing: a mental block from my childhood experiences with dogs. Paul never knows quite what to do with a wife awash in feelings, but one evening he patiently listened while I told him my stories. We would pick up a free puppy somewhere and irresponsibly let it fend for itself until it chased cars and we got tired of it, and then we would get rid of it. Worst was the time I saw my brother attempt to put down a dog behind the barn; it didn't die until the second shot. I'm sure Paul didn't have a clue what to say next, but he said exactly the right thing: "I promise we will never shoot a dog."

"Okay. Fine. Let's get the dog."

Paul built a nice fenced dog run. Daniel Fenske and his wife bathed the dog and gave us his doghouse, a leash, and a large bag of dog food.

Hansie came home on Thanksgiving Day. Already, he seems to belong here. His German name fits right in with Katzie's. I go out and talk to him in my native German dialect, and he understands me better than anyone else in the family does. I still am not a dog person, honestly, but I find him a very remarkable dog. I take pictures to post on my Web site, and it looks like I have a normal-sized dog and really little kids.

When we gave Steven the gift of a family, we had no idea what precious gifts he would give us in return. Thanks to him, we have a noble-looking German shepherd named Hansie who lies in his kennel and watches alertly over this new kingdom of his. He and the boys race around the yard together. He goes on walks with the girls and I know that no other dog, human, or cougar would dare come close enough to harm them. He loves us all, especially Steven, with a warm and gentle and mysterious affection.

About the Author

*D*orcas Smucker, a mother of six and a Mennonite minister's wife, lives in a 95-year-old farmhouse near Harrisburg, Oregon. In addition to her normal responsibilities of pulling splinters, settling arguments, and mopping floors, she writes a column, "Letter from Harrisburg" for the Eugene, Oregon, *Register-Guard*. She also speaks to various groups, which she enjoys because everyone listens and no one interrupts.

Her interests and hobbies include reading, crafts, sewing, travel, and exploring the Internet. She is the author of *Ordinary Days: Family Life in a Farmhouse*, also published by Good Books.

If you would like Dorcas Smucker to speak to your group . . .

Dorcas Smucker speaks to groups from time to time as her schedule permits. If you would like to invite her, simply write to her at letterfromhburg@juno.com.

Here's what some have said...

"We had people coming into the Library asking when she will speak again; her book flies off the shelves. She has been singled out as one of the favorite authors we have had. Her humor and insight speak to all faiths, nationalities, and sexes."
— *Friends of the Junction City Library*

"Dorcas was excellent and talked to a full house. The evaluations of her presentation, from those who attended, were 'A+.'"
— *Program Planner for OASIS, a senior-learning organization*

"Dorcas speaks from her heart in a gentle, honest way that resonates with her listeners. She speaks much like she writes."
— *Oregon Christian Writers Program Coordinator*

"I invited Dorcas to speak to my third-grade class on writing. Her presentation was outstanding! She had 60 third-grade students enthralled for over 30 minutes. She had an instant rapport with the group, and we will definitely invite her back."
— *Teacher at Spring Creek Elementary School*

Also by Dorcas Smucker

Ordinary Days
Family Life in a Farmhouse
155 pages • $9.95, paperback
ISBN: 978-1-56148-522-2

Table of Contents